D0122212

Psychotherapy with Psychotherapists

Florence W. Kaslow, a PH.D. from Bryn Mawr College, is in independent practice as a therapist and consultant in West Palm Beach, Florida. She is also Director of the Florida Couples and Family Institute and is an adjunct professor in the Department of Psychiatry at Duke University Medical School.

Dr. Kaslow was a professor and Chief of the Forensic Psychology/Psychiatry Section at Hahnemann Medical University in Philadelphia from 1973–1980. She also served there as Codirector of the PH.D./J.D. program in psychology and law, which Hahnemann cosponsored with Villanova Law School. She served as the first President of the American Board of Forensic Psychology, Inc. from 1978–1980.

Dr. Kaslow was Editor-in-chief of the *Journal of Marital and Family Therapy* from 1977 through 1981 and is currently on its editorial board and on the editorial boards of *Marriage & Family Review*, *Journal of Sex and Marital Therapy*, *Family Relations*, *Conciliation Courts Review*, *Journal of Divorce*, and both the Italian and the Argentinian *Journal of Family Therapy*. She has edited and coauthored books on supervision and consultation and on family therapy, has contributed chapters to many other books, and has had over sixty articles on a wide range of mental health and forensic topics published in professional journals.

Dr. Kaslow is a Diplomate in Clinical Psychology of the American Board of Professional Psychology (ABPP), a Diplomate in Forensic Psychology of the American Board of Forensic Psychology (ABFP), a Diplomate in Family Psychology of the American Board of Family Psychology (ABFAMP), and a Fellow of the American Psychological Association (APA). She has traveled extensively throughout the United States and numerous other countries including Norway, Japan, South Africa, Canada, Israel, and England conducting workshops and lecturing. She is a frequent guest on radio and TV shows in the United States.

Psychotherapy with Psychotherapists

Florence W. Kaslow, PH.D.
Editor

The Haworth Press
New York

Selections from *The Seasons of a Man's Life*, by Daniel J. Levinson *et al*, appearing in Chapter 8, have been reprinted by permission of Alfred A. Knopf, Inc., copyright 1978.

The Haworth Press, Inc., 28 East 22 Street, New York, New York 10010

Library of Congress Cataloging in Publication Data
Main entry under title:

Psychotherapy with psychotherapists.

Includes bibliographies and index.
1. Psychotherapists—Mental health. 2. Psychotherapists—Counseling of. 3. Psychotherapy patients.
I. Kaslow, Florence Whiteman. [DNLM: 1. Psychotherapy—Methods. WM 420 P97595]
RC451.4.P79P79 1984   616.89'023   83-18655
ISBN 0-86656-207-9

Printed in the United States of America

Contents

v

Contributors

John E. Churchill, M.S.W., is Chief of the Hypnotherapy (Outpatient) Clinic, Departments of Mental Health and Social Work, Wilford Hall USAF Medical Center, Lackland Air Force Base, Texas.

Erich Coché, PH.D., is a clinical psychologist in independent practice in Philadelphia and is a clinical associate professor at Hahnemann University, Philadelphia. He is a Diplomate in Clinical Psychology, American Board of Professional Psychology.

Judith Coché, PH.D., is a partner in Coché and Coché, a joint practice in clinical psychology. She is also clinical assistant professor, Hahnemann University, Philadelphia, Pennsylvania.

Allen Fay, M.D., is in the Department of Psychiatry, Mount Sinai School of Medicine, City University of New York.

Diane Friedman, PH.D., is a senior clinician at Community Mental Health Organization, Inc., Englewood, New Jersey.

Samuel Greenberg, M.D. is an analyst and a professor in the Department of Psychiatry, University of Florida, College of Medicine, Gainesville, Florida.

Florence W. Kaslow, PH.D., is in independent practice as a therapist and consultant in West Palm Beach, Florida. She is Director of the Florida Couples Family Institute and an adjunct professor in the Department of Psychiatry at Duke University Medical School, Durham, North Carolina.

Nadine J. Kaslow, PH.D., is an assistant Professor of Psychology in Psychiatry, Yale University School of Medicine, New Haven, Connecticut.

Arnold A. Lazarus, PH.D., is a professor in the Graduate School of Applied and Professional Psychology, Rutgers-The State University of New Jersey, New Brunswick.

William G. Neville, ED.D., is co-owner and Director of General Mediation and Arbitration Service, Inc., of Atlanta, Georgia. He is on the advisory boards of the Family Mediation Association and the Denver Custody Mediation Research Project.

Kenneth M. Padach, M.D., is a resident in Psychiatry at Cedars-Sinai Medical Center, Los Angeles, California.

Foreword

Theodore Blau, PH.D.

Although pursuing therapy with therapists has always been considered an essential aspect of psychoanalytic training, relatively few therapists have had the experience of pursuing therapy with therapists. This is not to say that such does not occur. As Florence Kaslow points out in the *Preface,* certain therapists are sought out by other therapists during times of difficulty. It is the unusual therapist, however, who seeks therapeutic intervention for himself or herself comfortably or easily. To many therapists this constitutes "failure." As the physician abhors illness, the therapist sees unsureness, self-doubt and confusion as marks of inadequacy and even a kind of therapist "sinfulness."

Conducting psychotherapy with another therapist is perhaps the greatest challenge to any mental health professional. The usual devices often used by psychotherapists to create a comfort zone within the very intense context of psychotherapy ordinarily are ineffective (as perhaps they should be) when working with other therapists. Prestige, psychological distance, professional status, psychotherapeutic language and other forms of mumbo jumbo are ludicrous in a therapist-therapist interaction.

One of the cardinal responsibilities of the effective therapist is to create a sanctuary, a place of such safety and confidentiality that the unthinkable can be thought and discussed. Difficult as this may be with the multitude of patients who seek our services, it is most difficult with the psychotherapist. This is particularly true with the psychotherapist who in some way has been unsuccessful because of his or her own emotional barriers and filters. I find no patient as distrustful as the unhappy, help-seeking psychotherapist. All of the skill and experience of a psychotherapist is required with regularity when conducting psychotherapy with another psychotherapist.

As the number of psychotherapists increase, this particular interaction is bound to increase. Conducting psychotherapy is a stressful and demanding profession, and the need for intervention to resolve consequent conflicts is bound to grow.

The time for this book is past due. Those who have been conducting psychotherapy with psychotherapists will find much to reassure and reinforce their own experience. Those who will be sought out professionally by their colleagues will find themselves far ahead of those of us who had to engineer our own solutions to the difficult interactions described in this book.

Theodore H. Blau, PH.D.
Tampa, Florida
December 1983

Preface

Florence Kaslow, PH.D.

Why in any community that has scores of therapists are only some sought out by other therapists? What variables are the decisive ones in this selection process? If therapists constitute the cognoscenti in the aggregate of consumers of mental health services, then the factors that affect their choices should shed light on the larger population of participants in psychotherapy.

Several years ago when I relocated from Pennsylvania to Florida, I found that rapidly a sizable portion of my patient population was comprised of other therapists—as individuals, as one part of a marital dyad, or as a member of a family unit seeking treatment. It was as part of the quest to ascertain why and how this occurred that the idea for this volume germinated. I invited each of the contributing authors to discuss this question—taking into consideration such factors as the therapist's reputation, theoretical persuasion, age, personality, style, and activities, in addition to such clinical practices as teaching, writing, supervising, and consulting. Beyond that, they were to freely associate to the question and utilize any combinations of impressionistic data, clinically based research data, questionnaires, responses, and survey of the literature as source material in producing their manuscripts. One of the objectives of this book is to provide a provocative beginning dialogue on this complex and intriguing phenomenon.

Starting with some assumptions based on my own clinical experience and on analytic discussions with other therapists, I selected some authors because of their acknowledged expertise in either a particular theory and technique of therapy (such as Fay and Lazarus in multimodal therapy) or in an interventive modality (such as Erich and Judith Coché in group therapy). To lend a balanced perspective, two articles were sought from the vantage point of the younger generation of clinicians in training: Padach, a resident in psychiatry and N. Kaslow and Friedman—both doctoral candidates completing their graduate work in psychology at the time these manuscripts were originally written. Intent on presenting a comprehensive and generic overview that encompasses the various specialties, I sought papers from individuals who practice one or more of the following: social work, psychology, psychiatry, psychoanalysis, marriage and family therapy, group therapy, hypnotherapy, and divorce mediation. Repeated themes (boundary issues, role modeling, transference and countertransference issues, and didactic therapy vs. therapy for intrapsychic and interpersonal difficulties) are elaborated and interrelated in the editorial commentaries that follow each chapter.

I give my sincere thanks to each of the contributing authors. In becoming involved in this project, they have risked sharing their own personal philosophy and/or therapeutic approach—in some cases knowing in advance that they are taking a more radical stance than is customary and may be severely criticized. Thanks also to Bill Cohen and Faye Zucker at The Haworth Press for their role in bringing this book to fruition. And as always, to my husband, Sol, my gratitude, for his encouragement of and patience with my world of work.

Psychotherapy with Psychotherapists

1

The Therapist in Behavioral and Multimodal Therapy

Allen Fay, M.D.
Arnold A. Lazarus, PH.D.

Starting from a traditional psychoanalytic perspective, we gradually shifted our orientations in a more behavioral direction and subsequently evolved a multimodal approach to assessment and treatment (Lazarus, 1981; Fay & Lazarus, 1981). It is not the purpose of this chapter to discuss in detail the practice of behavior therapy or multimodal therapy; the purpose is rather to indicate what might be distinctive about therapy with professionals, particularly from a behavioral or multimodal perspective. For readers unacquainted with behavior therapy, we define it as:

1. A philosophy that stresses learning as a major factor in the development and/or alleviation of a large proportion of dysfunctional behaviors, thought patterns, and feeling states, and
2. A set of techniques basically derived from and utilizing learning principles.

A close relationship to scientific methodology has been an intrinsic part of behavior therapy since its inception. The approach is essentially direct and problem focused.

The fundamental assumptions and distinguishing features of multimodal therapy have been summarized as follows (Lazarus & Fay, in press):

1. Psychological disorders represent some combination of biological determinants and learning factors.

1

2. Abnormal behavior that is a product of learning factors is acquired and maintained according to the same principles as normal behavior.

3. Dysfunctions attributable to faulty or inadequate learning, and even many disturbances with strong biological inputs, may be alleviated by the application of techniques derived from learning principles.

4. Presenting problems are viewed as real problems, and are investigated on their own merits, rather than being regarded as symptoms of some underlying problem or process.

5. The focus is on the present rather than on remote antecedents or unconscious processes. Immediate antecedents and current factors maintaining behavior are emphasized.

6. Assessment involves investigation of all areas of behavioral, cognitive, and interpersonal functioning to discover dysfunctions or deficits that are not immediately presented.

7. Simple behavioral descriptions are preferred to diagnostic labels.

8. Though recognizing that therapy, to some extent, involves transmission of values, behavior therapists minimize value statements. Rather than behavior being labeled as good or bad, its consequences are specified.

9. The therapist is active and interactive, often assuming the role of teacher and serving as a model.

10. The locus of resistance is primarily in the therapy and the therapist rather than in the patient.

11. Emphasis is on self-management. Patients are taught specific self-management techniques so that the likelihood of autonomous functioning in problem areas is maximized and dependency on the therapist is reduced. Assigned homework is an essential part of the behavioral approach.

12. Involvement of the identified patient's social network is desirable and often necessary. It permits the therapist to structure an optimal reinforcement environment and to resolve interpersonal conflicts through such approaches as communication training and contracting. (For details of specific behavioral techniques, see Bellack & Hersen, 1977; Goldfried & Davison, 1976; Rimm & Masters, 1979; Wilson & O'Leary, 1980.)

The multimodal approach is broader and deeper than traditional behavior therapy. In addition to overt behavioral responses, it delves into affective processes, sensory reactions, images, cognitions, and the subjective nuances of interpersonal relationships. There is significant overlap between behavioral and multimodal theories and techniques (Wilson, 1982), but there are also important points of departure (Lazarus, 1981, 1983). In most instances, when colleagues have sought our counsel, they were drawn to us partly for what we represent, as well as for what we oppose—psychodynamic psychotherapy (Lazarus & Fay, 1982; Fay & Lazarus, 1982).

In a much misquoted paper, Lazarus (1971a) observed that many behavior therapists were apt to seek treatment from nonbehavioral practitioners. This was *not* because these therapists had little confidence in behavioral techniques and considered psychoanalysis or Gestalt therapy or any other nonbehavioral system superior. Rather, since traditional behavior therapy has little to offer the person who functions well (i.e., is not phobic, obsessive-compulsive, unassertive, sexually dysfunctional, depressed, obese, or beset by maladaptive habits), it is logical to consult nonbehavioral clinicians when the object is to attain insight, to explore the "collective unconscious," to experience existential encounters, to enjoy an excursion in guided imagery, and so forth.

Our colleagues—psychiatrists, clinical psychologists, psychiatric social workers, counselors, and other mental health workers—have usually consulted us only after receiving more traditional therapy without success. The majority were self-referred, having read our writings or having attended lectures, seminars, or workshops that we presented. Their range of problems has covered the gamut from organic disorders, through substance abuse, schizophrenia, and major affective disorders, to anxiety, psychosexual dysfunctions, and family relationship issues. Rarely have we had the experience of treating a colleague who simply wished to get in touch with his or her feelings, or understand his or her dreams. In terms of DSM III nomenclature, the most benign subsets were comprised of colleagues with "adjustment disorders with work or academic inhibition," with specific "marital problems," and with "other specified family circumstances."

The vulnerability of mental health professionals to psychological-psychiatric ills is well documented and the high suicide rate among psychiatrists well publicized (Freeman, 1967; Rich & Pitts, 1980). Still the idea persists in the public mind, and even among professionals, that therapists have, or at least should have, a high level of psychological wellness. This attitude tends to make it difficult for some therapists to seek assistance, and it may complicate therapy as well.

During the first year of psychiatric residence one of us (A.F.) recalls how anxiety-producing it was when on several occasions a psychiatrist was admitted to our inpatient service. Although a senior attending psychiatrist was usually the principal therapist, a resident was involved as well, and on occasion a resident was *the* therapist. How does one talk to such a patient? How does a tyro talk to a seasoned clinician, let alone be therapeutic? Fortunately, the therapist-patients were usually not as forbidding as the residents had anticipated. Admittedly, this situation is somewhat unusual in that therapists generally seek help from equally or, often, more experienced therapists than themselves.

Another trauma occurred when a fellow resident had a psychotic episode. Twenty years ago it was de rigeur for residents to be in psychoanalysis, and somehow if you were accepted for treatment by a training analyst at a major institute, it seemed to offer some kind of assurance that psychosis was not in your future. Being in psychotherapy as opposed to analysis was a mark of inferiority. Behavior therapy was not even accorded the status of heresy; it was simply superficial nonsense. As time passed, it became more apparent that therapists were as vulnerable as anyone else to psychiatric disability, and possibly more so. In fact it became clear that some enter our field seemingly in search of help, whereas others do so in an attempt to demonstrate that they are not disturbed.

In our first year of training, a junior staff psychiatrist made the astounding statement that he never saw a patient whose symptom he did not have himself to some degree (Fay, 1978). What seemed like a shocking and inappropriate revelation of gross psychopathology was seen subsequently as one of the central truths in the practice of psychological therapy. What this young psychiatrist meant was that most individuals, at some time or another, have irrational fears, depressive ideation, superstitious ruminations, compulsions, thoughts of suicide, and paranoid notions. One of the senior supervisors, who was a faculty member of an analytic institute, commented that when candidates came for a training analysis, one of the most important aspects of the therapy was to convince them that they were neurotic and not simply satisfying a perfunctory requirement.

In most essential respects, our therapy is identical for professionals and nonprofessionals. Assessment procedures are no different, the technical armamentarium is basically the same, and relationship factors are crucial to both. But there are significant differences although we cannot generalize about therapy with "therapists." Therapists have different theoretical orientations and styles in their practices, and they have different expectations and beliefs about therapy for themselves. Some therapist-patients (we refer to them as t-ps for convenience) are absolutely committed to therapy as a way of life and seem totally comfortable consulting a colleague. Others are embarrassed and feel less worthy as a result of their excursion into therapy. Still others who had therapy or psychoanalysis earlier in life feel that it is a defeat to seek help again.

Initially, our major thrust of therapy is usually in the cognitive sphere; there are certain basic beliefs and attitudes that require examination and modification. For example, we regard the idea that therapists are, or should be, better than their clients as highly dysfunctional (Lazarus & Fay, 1975). The basic difference between therapists and nontherapists is *not* pathology, neither the fact nor even the degree; the basic difference is training and experience in their vocational area. Consider the following dialogue between Fay (A.F.) and a 41-year-old female t-p:

T-P: Yesterday I saw a patient who was so much like me, it was scary. It's really a joke, the blind leading the blind.
A.F.: Who's more appropriate?
T-P: Who? A normal person.
A.F.: What's a "normal person"?
T-P: You know.
A.F.: You mean someone well–adjusted who sailed through the best schools without a care, someone with a great marriage, fabulous sex life, two normal children who never had a problem, makes $200,000 a year, someone who is never anxious and never depressed and never has self-doubts? Is that what you mean?
T-P: Yeah, something like that.
A.F.: I'd be terrified to see someone like that. I don't think I could learn anything—or relate to such a person.
T-P: But I'm a far cry from that.
A.F.: Tell me, how many patients have you destroyed with your problems?

T-P: *(Laughs)* I hope not too many.

A.F.: Do you know what to do for this patient who is so similar to you?

T-P: I think so.

A.F.: Are you interested in helping her?

T-P: Sure!

A.F.: Does she seem to trust you?

T-P: I guess so.

A.F.: Are your problems bothering her?

T-P: Not that I know. Actually, when I told her how devastated I was when Bill left me, she was relieved.

A.F.: *(Paradoxically)* Well, then, it seems that you have all the ingredients of a terrible therapist.

T-P: *(Laughs)*

A.F.: Apart from the fact that you're not quite as dilapidated as you think, did it ever occur to you that mental health might not be the most important quality in a good therapist? You know, Freud was a complete fruitcake.

The type of problem and the intensity of symptoms certainly may be a factor in a therapist's ability to conduct a practice. For example, one must be able to tolerate criticism from patients and be reasonably comfortable when discussing sex. Depression in a therapist may make it more difficult to communicate than would a circumscribed phobia or hypochondriasis. On the other hand, the latter symptoms might preclude the behavioral technique of in vivo exposure with participant modeling (i.e., the therapist takes the patient into the feared situation and demonstrates exposure or contamination exercises).

Among the unique relationship factors with t-ps is the fact that more experienced therapists who work with less experienced t-ps are not only communicating messages about problem solving but are also transmitting therapeutic skills. A large segment of our t-p population has consisted of graduate students in psychology. Here we are often seen as teachers as well as therapists, especially by those students in programs with a cognitive-behavioral orientation. A subset of this group consists of students who have been in our classes.

Another significant feature of our relationship with t-ps is that we will sometimes refer a patient to our t-p. Although some might think that this would complicate the "transference," even orthodox analysts have engaged in this practice since Freud's time. In fact, many years ago one of us (A.F.) was treating a patient jointly with his analyst, an orthodox Freudian on the faculty of the New York Psychoanalytic Institute. Referring patients to t-ps might create problems if you are known to engage in it with some t-ps and not others. More than one of our t-ps has said "If you didn't think I was too sick, you would have referred a patient to me" or "*You* wouldn't send me a patient, would you, and take the risk that I would louse it up?"

Sometimes the converse occurs, that is, our t-p refers a patient to us, either someone he or she is having difficulty with or perhaps a relative or friend.

A couple of t-ps have asked us to arrange our schedules so as to avoid waiting-room encounters. We can recall two occasions over the years when patients showed up at the wrong times. In one case it was assumed that the t-p's session was a conference between colleagues, and in the other case it was not mentioned. As an aside, it is obvious that many professional psychotherapists who seek personal psychotherapy are even more sensitive than "ordinary patients" about matters of confidentiality. Some of our psychoanalytically oriented confreres particularly have been concerned that nobody should discover that they sought our professional counsel.

Behaviorally oriented t-ps will often know the techniques we suggest, so that the major task is to get them to implement what they already know; whereas with nonprofessionals we must explain the basic approach as well as describe and illustrate the techniques.

In our experience, one of the most essential factors in therapy is therapist self-disclosure. It is particularly important with t-ps, because we are even more likely to be role models for such patients. As mentioned earlier, behavior therapy rests on learning principles and the techniques derived therefrom, and modeling is one of the major mechanisms of learning (Bandura, 1969). It is a tenet of social learning theory that the closer the resemblance between the subject and model, the easier it is for learning to occur. T-ps are sometimes encouraged to be more disclosing to their own patients for the dual reason that it is often beneficial to themselves and their patients. Although there is some controversy in this area, coping models are probably more effective than mastery models, so that telling patients about our great successes in life and our sterling achievements will not be as effective as discussions about our own struggles with some of the issues with which they are dealing. We disclose our own symptoms, limitations, and life problems, not compulsively but selectively, when we feel it would serve a constructive purpose for the patient.

There is a tendency for many patients to put therapists in a one-up position; t-ps may do this also, even while trying to convince us of their adequacy. It is critical for the therapists of professionals not to feel competitive, or act in a competitive way, or derive satisfaction from the plight of their colleagues, or feel superior to them.

Two patients expressed concern that we would steal their ideas and publish them. Trust may be even more important when working with t-ps than with others, since betrayal can have professional as well as personal repercussions.

Some feel that professionals in therapy know too much and that their expertise fosters "resistance." We have discussed the concept of *resistance as rationalization* elsewhere (Lazarus & Fay, 1982; Fay & Lazarus, 1982). Some years ago, a very scholarly confrere was told by his world-renowned analyst that if he continued reading the analytic literature his therapy could not continue. In behavior therapy, as a rule, the more you know, the *better* it is. Although in some instances this attitude may foster intellectual discussions about therapy, it also makes it easier to discuss basic issues and implement techniques. Frequently, a therapy session is a combination of therapy and supervision. In fact, we believe that supervision is often part of the therapy, since discussions about therapy and specific issues in case management can be personally helpful. In general, supervision may be therapeutic, provided the supervisor has the appropriate personality and style. T-ps may feel better and develop greater self-confidence and self-esteem by improving their technical competence.

One patient reported that work inhibition was one of her major problems. She mentioned that she had been thinking about writing a book, but had procrastinated for several years. We talked about her most important and interesting topic for a while, and then she was asked to mail an outline to us before the next session, which she did. This occurred at the same time that one of us was working on a book. He commented that his way of writing was to take a week off several times during the year and devote it to full-time writing. The patient thought that was a good idea and called a couple of days later to say that she would be taking the following week off. At the end of the period she came in with about 45 pages of typed material. We sometimes make specific content suggestions and even edit the writings of some of our patients. Occasionally we have asked a patient to do the same for us.

Sometimes therapists feel that it is a sign of weakness to be in therapy more than other patients do. Analytically oriented individuals are particularly harsh with themselves, making negative judgments about their behavior and labeling themselves immature, narcissistic, infantile, regressed, or acting out. The following dialogue between a 36-year-old clinical psychologist (c.p.) and Lazarus (a.a.l.) illustrates this point:

c.p.: I'm so damn immature and controlling. So *needy*.

a.a.l.: Can you give me some examples?

c.p.: All right, let's talk about the set-up at work. When I joined the hospital, the Adolescent Unit was losing money. So I was put in charge, and within six to seven months they were out of the red and showing a nice profit. Well, the chairman never said anything about it, and I kept waiting to see if he would say, "Nice work!" or something like that, some acknowledgment. Now, why the hell do I need his approval? I should be more mature and secure instead of looking for strokes from Big Daddy. Why do I have to suckle the breast?

a.a.l.: I don't see anything wrong with a desire for recognition and reward for one's efforts. Why is that a symptom of immaturity?

c.p.: Well, when he said nothing to me about the—if I say so myself—fantastic job I had done, I got pissed and asked for a raise. It's the same theme—give to me, nurture me, stroke me. I see the patients exploiting, controlling, manipulating all the time, but I'm no different. I'm just as regressive and immature.

a.a.l.: So in your book, a mature individual wouldn't desire rewards or recognition?

c.p.: Self-satisfaction should suffice. I know I did a hell of a good job. I pulled them out of a hole. I feel good about that. So why be so hung up on whether or not others applaud or appreciate my efforts or achievements? It's this damn dependency.

A.A.L.: You seem to put negative labels on everything. Self-satisfaction is sweetened by acknowledgment and reward from
others.

C.P.: Yes, but wait till you hear the rest of it. My request for a
raise was turned down. Well, when I learned this bit of information I was really down.

A.A.L.: Depressed?

C.P.: You bet! I just sulked around the place all day, behaving
exactly like any of the adolescents on the ward.

A.A.L.: Weren't you angry? Didn't you feel that you deserved the
raise?

C.P.: Who can figure out who deserves what? The point is that if
the chairman would have noticed or praised my efforts, I
wouldn't have asked for the raise—it was only when he
didn't give me the strokes that I asked for the money.

A.A.L.: Would you rather have received the strokes or the money?

C.P.: My immediate impulse was to say "both"! That's what I
mean about being needy.

A.A.L.: Are you implying that if you had received both lavish
praise and a raise, you still would have felt deprived or
shortchanged?

C.P.: Well, when people start gushing, I question their hidden
agendas.

A.A.L.: Let me rephrase the question. If you had received both acknowledgment for your achievements and a salary incre-
ment, would you still complain that you wished for more?

C.P.: No, that would be great, but my point is why be so put out
when it's not forthcoming?

A.A.L.: I think you have unrealistic expectations for yourself.
Moreover, your psychological orientation leads you to fall
back on global pejorative labels when your idealistic standards are compromised. Self-reward can go only so far,
and when appreciation from significant others is not forthcoming, I maintain that there is nothing pathological in
feeling let down. What also strikes me about your account
is that you made no assertive responses. You did not approach the chairman and ask him if he was aware of the
fact that your efforts had changed the ward from veritable
bankruptcy to one of financial profit.

C.P.: But that would be so controlling!

C.P.'s deprecatory talents seemed unlimited. He was able to pull "primitive impulse gratifications" out of thin air the way magicians pull cards, coins, and rabbits from hats. The outcome was inevitable self-condemnation. (The corollary is that such a therapist might be apt to engender guilt and self-belittlement in his clients.)

Whereas many of our psychoanalytically oriented patients tended to dwell on putative complexes and would often allude to intrapsychic dynamics (thereby retarding the course of therapy), the same tendencies, but with different words, were prevalent in other nonbehaviorally trained clinicians. For example, those with a systems orientation tended to perceive double-binds, hidden agendas, sabotaging maneuvers, and various triangulations and collusions. It was often impossible to detect precise behavioral referents for these inferred constructs. We are not denying that nonconscious processes may determine certain behaviors, that defensive reactions may lead to various perceptual distortions, and that some communication patterns are governed by manipulative ploys and unhealthy collusions. Our point is that many of our colleague-patients tended to perceive pathologies in themselves that appeared to have no basis in fact.

Psychiatrists or other physicians, when treated by a clinical psychologist (or any nonmedical therapist), sometimes present barriers pertaining to the medical hegemony. Psychiatrists wield more power and authority than psychologists, and it is not uncommon for physicians to "pull rank" when treatment issues prove threatening. One of us (A.A.L.) was treating a psychiatrist who manifested persecutory trends, a distinct loosening of associations, and signs of inappropriate affect. The advisability of consulting another psychiatrist to determine if psychotropic medication might be indicated was tactfully broached. The following dialogue (reconstructed from memory) ensued:

CLIENT: What gives you the right to talk about drugs to me? Do you like to play doctor with all your patients? I've a good mind to have your license revoked. Let me remind you that I majored in psychology at college, after which I went to medical school, and then I went through a residency in psychiatry. And you have the gall to come on to me like some wise and seasoned physician when you know noth-

ing about medicine! If I needed medicine, I sure as hell
would be able to recognize it before you would.

A.A.L.:   It's difficult to be objective with oneself. As you know, the
right medication can often potentiate important
behavioral changes.

CLIENT: I can prescribe my own medication. I don't need you to
tell me about that.

A.A.L.:   I'd be happier if you were willing to give over that responsibility to another psychiatrist. It's like a dentist refusing
to see a colleague and insisting on filling his own teeth.

In the foregoing excerpt many issues other than the medical
versus nonmedical emphasis are present, among which the client's
anxieties and unwillingness to recognize the extent of his own limitations are perhaps uppermost.

When working with a thirty-four-year-old psychiatrist who referred himself for the treatment of "anxiety-hysteria," Lazarus
(1971b), during the second interview, asked him to project himself
into the following scene: "Imagine that you and I are on a deserted
island for six months with two beautiful women, one of whom will
be attracted and responsive only to you, whereas the other will be
turned on only by me, so there is no risk of rejection or any need
for competition." The following dialogue shows how productive
this fantasy test can be, both diagnostically and therapeutically:

PATIENT: Oh, God! The four of us will be there for six months?

A.A.L.:   Uh huh.

PATIENT: Ummmm, uh. Gee! Well, I will obviously be in charge of
our physical well-being, you know. I'll obviously be the
doctor.

A.A.L.:   That's taken care of. I mean it's a magic island, and we
are all going to be well and healthy for the entire period.
We won't require your medical services, just you as a
human being.

PATIENT: Well, somebody has to be in charge of the place. We
won't let the women take over, so obviously you and I
will have to compete for leadership.

A.A.L.:   Why? I mean, why can't we just all be together as four
human beings—sharing, experiencing, confiding, relating? Why must someone be in charge?

PATIENT: I just know you'll tell me what and what not to do. And
I'll kick you in the balls.

A.A.L.: Would requests or suggestions be tantamount to telling you what to do?

PATIENT: I can be awful touchy. But let's face it. Even though you have ruled out competition between us and the women, I might still feel that your woman was closer and more loving to you than mine was to me. This would cause friction between my uh . . . girl and myself, uh . . . and also lead to jealousy and resentment toward you.

A.A.L.: It sounds as if you are just determined to look for trouble and to find deficiencies in yourself. You set yourself up so that everything becomes a competition. Couldn't you just enjoy your relationship and not even notice if I was a little closer or perhaps a little more distant from my woman? Obviously, if there was a big difference, if my woman was much more loving and attentive to me than yours was to you . . .

PATIENT: How much is "much more"? Look, frankly, I'd be afraid that I wouldn't be as adequate sexually as you would be.

A.A.L.: In what way?

PATIENT: Well, in real life, my wife has only slept with me, so she has no means of comparison. But maybe the girl on the island has had many lovers, and I wouldn't measure up.

As the dialogue continued, the focus of therapy centered on his anxiety, extreme competitiveness, and sexual insecurity. The course of therapy was surprisingly smooth, although from time to time his competitive proclivities intruded into the therapeutic relationship, calling for frank yet tactful management. Whenever he felt threatened, he tended to fall back on his M.D. degree.

We have seen many couples in marital therapy where one or both partners were mental health professionals. It is our clinical impression that when *both* were therapists, with few exceptions, marriage therapy was more easily conducted than with nonprofessionals. On the other hand, where one party was a therapist, couples therapy tended to prove more difficult. One of the most prevalent tactics in the latter instance was the use of jargon by the t-p against the partner. This called for considerable clinical skill in recognizing the professional credentials of the t-p and simultaneously supporting the nonprofessional partner against unfair onslaughts.

Some of the most challenging treatment situations arose when multimodal assessment dictated the need for family retraining and where one or more family members were themselves professional therapists. The family setting tended to bring competitive strivings into the open. In some instances, the therapist family member was inclined to demonstrate for his or her family that he or she was "the best therapist in the room." In other families, the primary allegiance of a sibling, or especially a child of the therapist family member, led to combative tactics whenever we made observations or suggestions. When recommending homework exercises to enhance communication in one family, the eleven-year-old son of the t-p (a prominent psychotherapist) said: "I don't have to listen to you. My dad knows more than you do!"

A few colleagues have consulted us to confirm their allegiance to the safe confines of the couch. They labelled our educational orientation as "mechanistic" and retreated to the introspectionistic realms of psychoanalysis. We have found this especially frustrating when we felt fairly certain that if only the t-p would be willing to modify certain behaviors, positive benefits would accrue. In many instances, this apparent "resistance" proved to be a function of the t-p's a priori belief that all overt behavior is an insignificant part of a more basic unconscious conflict. Elsewhere (Lazarus & Fay, 1975) we have emphasized that "many people waste inordinate amounts of time struggling to change by delving into their early life, by analyzing their dreams, by reading ponderous tomes, and through philosophical reflections about the meaning of life. Life is too short and that struggle too long."

Behavior therapy and especially multimodal therapy are freer from the taboos and proscriptions that typify some approaches to psychotherapy. For example, when one of us had just started analysis, he grew tense at the sight of his analyst sitting a few rows away at a professional meeting, because he did not know whether he would be greeted cordially or viewed as complicating the transference. We are generally delighted to see t-ps at meetings and sometimes exchange information about interesting conferences and workshops either of us may not have heard about. At times, t-ps attend presentations where we are the speakers.

Modern behavior therapy and multimodal therapy are, above all, humanistic endeavors. Theodore Kheel, the well-known labor negotiator, said that "some people think in terms of problems and some in terms of solutions." Our treatment orientation is essentially one of *problem solving*, and no matter who the client or patient turns out to be, we do our best to ensure that he or she will acquire a more adaptive repertoire of coping skills.

References

Bandura, A. *Principles of behavior modification*. New York: Holt, Rinehart & Winston, 1969.

Bellack, A. S., & Hersen, M. *Behavior modification: An introductory textbook*. Baltimore: Williams & Wilkins, 1977.

Fay, A. *Making things better by making them worse*. New York: Hawthorn Books, 1978.

Fay, A., & Lazarus, A. A. Multimodal therapy and the problems of depression. In J. F. Clarkin & H. I. Glazer (Eds.), *Depression: Behavioral and directive intervention strategies*. New York: Garland, 1981.

Fay, A., & Lazarus, A. A. Psychoanalytic resistance and behavioral nonresponsiveness: A dialectical impasse. In P. L. Wachtel (Ed.), *Resistance: Psychodynamic and behavioral approaches*. New York: Plenum, 1982.

Freeman, W. Psychiatrists who kill themselves: A study in suicide. *American Journal of Psychiatry*, 1967, 124, 846–847.

Goldfried, M. R., & Davison, G. C. *Clinical behavior therapy*. New York: Holt, Rinehart & Winston, 1976.

Lazarus, A. A. Where do behavior therapists take their troubles? *Psychological Reports*, 1971a, 28, 349–350.

Lazarus, A. A. *Behavior therapy and beyond*. New York: McGraw-Hill, 1971b.

Lazarus, A. A. *The practice of multimodal therapy*. New York: McGraw-Hill, 1981.

Lazarus, A. A. Multimodal therapy. In R. J. Corsini (Ed.), *Current psychotherapies*. (3rd ed.) Itasca, Illinois: Peacock, 1983.

Lazarus, A. A., & Fay, A. *I can if I want to*. New York: Warner Books, 1975.

Lazarus, A. A., & Fay, A. Resistance or rationalization? A cognitive-behavioral perspective. In P. L. Wachtel (Ed.), *Resistance: Psychodynamic and behavioral approaches*. New York: Plenum, 1982.

Lazarus, A. A., & Fay, A. Behavior therapy. *American Psychiatric Association Commission on Psychiatric Therapies* (in press).

Rich, C. L., & Pitts, F. N. Suicide by psychiatrists: A study of medical specialists among 18,730 consecutive physician deaths during a 5-year period, 1967–72. *Journal of Clinical Psychiatry*, 1980, 41, 261–263.

Rimm, D. C., & Masters, J. C. *Behavior therapy: Techniques and empirical findings*. (2nd ed.). New York: Academic Press, 1979.

Wilson, G. T. Clinical issues and strategies in the practice of behavior therapy. In C. M. Franks, G. T. Wilson, P. C. Kendall, & K. D. Brownell, *Annual review of behavior therapy*. Vol. 8. New York: Guilford, 1982.

Wilson, G. T., & O'Leary, K. D. *Principles of behavior therapy*. Englewood Cliffs, N.J.: Prentice-Hall, 1980.

EDITOR'S COMMENTARY

The Clarity and Definitiveness
of Multimodal Therapy

Fay and Lazarus succeed in elucidating with great specificity some
often-murky areas. Like N. Kaslow and Friedman (Chapter 3),
they deal with a client population that includes a subset of graduate students. Although their trainee populations were drawn from
somewhat different geographic areas and although they discuss
different treatment approaches (mainly psychodynamic and be-
havioral/multimodal), both pairs of authors indicate that the students may well receive from some clinicians therapy that includes
a component of supervision. This marks quite a departure from a
purist stance of a clear demarcation between these two functions.

In this chapter, Fay and Lazarus highlight how often the therapist becomes the prototypical "role model" of how therapy is
done—and even, perhaps, how it should be done. Training and
training issues may become intertwined with treatment and treatment issues; thus a complex tapestry emerges as these roles overlap. When the patient/trainee is also a student in the therapist's
classes, apparently a not uncommon happening in small communities with a shortage of fine therapists who are not also on the faculty of the graduate or medical school, great caution must be exercised in keeping their roles and functions separate but integrated.
For example, how does the therapist's knowledge of a student's
deep deprivation impinge upon how he or she grades the student
in a course? Does the patient as student exploit the sympathy of
the therapist as professor? Does the therapist's power cross roles
and intimidate the student in some subtle ways or inhibit his or her
self-disclosures?

Given the therapist/professor's multidimensional influence,
the process of selecting graduate students and faculty becomes
compelling. Well-designed research to determine the impact of this
multiplicity of roles on the student's therapy and training certainly
seems crucial if we are to derive answers to these important questions.

Several additional aspects of the material presented by Fay
and Lazarus initially seem unusual, yet on further consideration

16

are probably not so atypical. They indicate that they sometimes refer potential patients to their own patients who are therapists, implying that they have confidence in their competence. Certainly
this may give a boost to the latter's self-esteem, yet one wonders if
it also heightens feelings of dependency and competitiveness.
They also indicate that they sometimes edit patients' writings and
have collegial relationships with patient/therapists at professional
conferences.

Given that in analytic circles, analyst and analysand are cau-
tioned that contact outside of the analytic hour will impede the
transference and is definitely contraindicated (see Chapter 2), this
work by Fay and Lazarus serves to highlight the diversity of ideas
about what is tenable, feasible, and appropriate in the field.

2

Psychoanalytic Treatment for Therapists, Residents, and Other Trainees

Samuel Greenberg, M.D.
Florence W. Kaslow, PH.D.

At the outset, let us briefly explain what we mean by psychoanalytic therapy (and recommend the reader to primary sources for a full articulation of the various theoretical foundations and perspectives in *The Collected Papers of Sigmund Freud* and the writings of Jung, Adler, Horney, Sullivan, Abraham, Greenson, Lang, and other more recent theoretician-therapists). There is no official definition of psychoanalysis. Many years ago a committee was appointed by the American Psychoanalytic Association to formulate a definition for use by that group. This committee struggled for several years, but could not decide on a definition that was acceptable. Nonetheless, it is generally agreed that psychoanalysis is a form of psychotherapy that concerns itself with the analysis of resistance and transference (Brenner, 1982). Its methodology involves free association, the interpretation of dreams and slips of the tongue, and seeking to bring about the return of repressed material by making the unconscious conscious (Waelder, 1964). For followers of the classical tradition, it means four sessions per week and the use of the couch by the patient. Classical analysts do not consider any other treatment to be analysis, but rather would label it analytically oriented psychotherapy.

For the neo-Freudians or culturalists, therapy three times a week, with the patient sitting up, also constitutes analysis. There continues to be a great deal of discussion regarding the boundary line between psychoanalysis and analytically oriented therapy. Some feel that the boundary between the two is sharp; others feel that it is blurred. A good overview of the problem was presented by Paolino (1981) in a recent article.

We believe that there is no sharp dichotomy and use the terms psychoanalysis, psychoanalytic therapy, and analytically oriented psychotherapy interchangeably. Our views are quite similar to those Portnoy articulated in the second edition of the *American Handbook of Psychiatry* (Portnoy, 1974). It is an uncovering form of therapy that takes place in the matrix of a unique and evolving relationship between the patient and the therapist. The goal is to bring about a basic and long-term change in the direction and quality of a person's life; to shift his or her energies from maintaining the neurotic system to healthy self-realization. "It is a reorientation through self-knowledge" (Horney, 1950). Overcoming resistances that prevent insight from emerging and the analysis of transference are the essential processes involved. Assessing the pattern of the patient's relationship to the analyst eventually constitutes the most important area for developing insight. The emphasis on analysis of the relationship should be primarily on the "here and now" rather than on the patient's distant past. We agree with Gill (1982) that if this is done, "analytic technique should be applicable over a broader range of settings, whether gauged by frequency of sessions, use of couch or chair, type of patient or experience of the therapist, than is usually considered possible." It is essentially a long-term therapy, but some shorter therapies, or time-limited therapies, may use analytic principles (Kadis & Markowitz, 1972). Restructuring of the personality is frequently one of the goals.

Mental health professionals are, for the most part, consistent. They practice what they preach. When they have problems in living, significant degrees of anxiety or depression, or other neurotic symptoms, they seek help from highly respected colleagues. Some go from the role of the therapist to the role of the patient quite easily and are not obstructed by feeling that there is a stigma attached to or a weakness of character evidenced by seeking therapeutic help. Their attitude is the same as for friends and neighbors who ask what to do about crises or neurotic problems: they suggest they commence therapy. They believe in what they are doing and they perceive therapy as a constructive measure that not only relieves symptoms but also leads to personal growth. Others who are more ambivalent about their chosen profession and do not wish to risk self-disclosure to an analyst will shy away from therapy and rationalize their decision.

THE THERAPIST AS PATIENT

Mental health professionals have several advantages over lay people when they enter therapy. They know which therapists are available in the community and so can make a better choice. They are familiar with the various schools of psychoanalytic thought and can choose a therapist with a compatible frame of reference—a classical Freudian, Jungian, Sullivanian, Horneyan, or Kleinian, among others—with whom they anticipate they will be able to establish a therapeutic alliance. Another advantage is that they know what the therapy process is likely to be and are better prepared for its vicissitudes. Almost always, they are intelligent and verbal. [EDITOR'S NOTE: See N. Kaslow and Friedman, Chapter 3, for more on the "ideal" patient.] For all these reasons, therapy is likely to start off well and end well, although there may be some precarious and despairing phases during the course of the analysis. Some know that no analysis is ever complete, and they set more reasonable goals for themselves. When these are achieved, they end with a feeling of accomplishment. Many therapists make "good" patients. Others who are perfectionistic and/or narcissistic may be chronically disgruntled and have great difficulty working through their resistance and giving up such defense mechanisms as denial, projection, and repression (A. Freud, 1971). Nothing involving human beings is simple, and analysis is indeed a complex process.

Although most clinicians probably fall in the "normal-neurotic" range, our ranks also include schizophrenics, borderline, and psychopathic personalities. These are always difficult patients to treat, and this is especially so when their clinical knowledge is used to reinforce their already formidable resistance. They may be highly manipulative, and the analyst may be especially vulnerable to their maneuvers, because he or she often tries to do even more for therapist-patients than for others. In our experience, it is valuable for the therapist to be clear about this and insist on treating them like any other patients. The therapist will have to set very firm guidelines and say to such patients, in effect, "You will be treated like all other patients, the fees will be my customary ones, and missed sessions will be paid for. I shall not intervene in any legal proceedings or appear before any boards on your behalf. If this is satisfactory then we can proceed." These patients can be quite destructive of the relationship unless dealt with firmly. Competitive strivings and boundary issues may also need to be addressed and worked through.

THE THERAPISTS' THERAPIST

In all fields there are special individuals who are sought out by their colleagues when they need help. There are lawyers' lawyers and doctors' doctors. And there are also therapists' therapists. These are people who have distinguished themselves by publications, lectures, and academic and clinical achievements. They enjoy a fine reputation among their colleagues. They find that their colleagues make interesting and rewarding patients and are pleased to be sought out by them. They like the idea that they may be having a favorable influence, not only on their patients, but on their patients' patients.

In the treatment of other mental health professionals, an interesting issue comes up: when is it treatment and when is it education or quasi-supervision (Kaslow, 1972)? In all fields of medicine, patients are educated to deal more effectively with their illness, whatever the ailment. However, in no field of medicine is treatment of such educational value as in psychoanalysis. This has long been acknowledged, and an extensive personal analysis is a required part of the curriculum of all recognized analytic institutes. Beginning with Freud himself, all of the psychoanalytic pioneers attracted psychiatrists and other clinicians, who came for treatment. They often went on to become distinguished analysts in their own right. The reverse holds true in that the therapist may feel that some colleagues are not suitable therapists, and this creates a dilemma, which we discuss further on in this chapter.

Until fairly recently only the largest cities had psychoanalytic institutes and an abundance of well-trained therapists. New York City, for example, has six analytic institutes and also many other centers for postgraduate education. It therefore has hundreds of outstanding therapists available to other mental health professionals. Boston, Chicago, Los Angeles, Philadelphia, and other large cities are similarly well endowed. This has not always been true for many medium-sized cities. Not so many years ago, Miami had only one qualified analyst in the city, and almost half the psychiatrists in town were analyzed by him. This condition has changed a great deal in the last decade, and there are now 400 psychiatrists and a psychoanalytic society and institute in Miami. In the past decade, the geographic distribution of analysts has improved, and even many small cities now have competent analysts.

Although some therapists like to treat their colleagues, others avoid doing so. There are often complications in treating other mental health professionals. The therapist-patient may be involved in legal proceedings, divorce and custody battles, and problems involving hospital staffs or boards of medical or psychological examiners. The analyst recognizes that such a patient will require more than treatment, that he or she wants an advocate as much as a therapist. These patients may involve the therapist in court hearings, depositions, or appearances before boards. All this is disruptive of a busy practice and may be alien to his or her concept of what an analyst should be and do.

There are many times and circumstances when prominent analysts are under pressure to accept a colleague as a patient. For example, a psychiatric resident may begin to act in a bizarre way; this comes to the attention of the chairman of the department, who then requests a faculty colleague to see the resident. Or the president of a county medical society may request that the analyst see some practitioner who has been accused of making sexual overtures to patients. It is a wise therapist who is not pressured into accepting a patient with whom he or she is likely to be uncomfortable or to form a negative countertransference. Fortunately, there are psychiatrists who do not mind court appearances or media publicity, and they may do well with such patients, finding them particularly interesting and challenging.

THE PSYCHIATRIC RESIDENT

Unfortunately, there is some truth to the degrading joke, "You don't have to be crazy to be a psychiatrist, but it helps." There is a higher incidence of suicide among psychiatrists than among other medical specialists. It is also true that some clinicians are interested in this field because they hope that in pursuing it they will come to understand or resolve some personal problems. Many plan on psychoanalysis for therapeutic as well as educational objectives. There are, however, some psychotherapists who are not conscious of their problems, or the extent of them, until they are triggered by exposure to psychiatric patients. It is well known that medical students and nurses are often disturbed by exposure to psychiatric patients. Some may leave the field as a result; others decide to get personal therapy and stay in the field. It is natural for some psychiatric residents to turn to a member of the attending staff or the faculty of the medical center where they are in training for assistance in exploring their inner world of fears, desires, pent up anger, sexual longings, confusion, ambivalences, etc. But others seek out someone at a distance, preferring to travel far and feel safe with an analyst not involved in their training program.

Older colleagues are usually quite sympathetic to these problems and are ready to provide help. If it is an acute disturbance, supportive therapy and not psychoanalysis is indicated at first. If, however, it is a long-standing personality disorder that has been stirred up, then psychoanalysis may well be the treatment of choice. If the medical center is in a fairly large city, there will be many analysts available. The resident will then become another regular patient. He or she will visit the analyst's private office, pay a fee that they agree upon, and in all ways become an ordinary patient. His or her privacy is safeguarded in all respects. If the medical center is in a small city, all the competent therapists may be members of the faculty, and their offices may be in the teaching hospital. It may be impossible to provide real privacy in these circumstances. It could be awkward for the patient to visit the therapist where secretaries and colleagues note the regular visits and infer that he or she is coming for treatment. To some residents this may present no problem, but to others it may be so distressing that the therapy is terminated soon.

There are other complications when the resident is being treated by a member of the faculty. The resident may hear tales about the therapist and may know a great deal about him or her from lectures, publications, and writings. This may be a hindrance to free association and full self-disclosure and may make the course of therapy more difficult, since it complicates the transference.

The reverse side is that the therapist may find current and former patients in the audience when giving lectures or participating in seminars or conferences. We have each spoken to groups of residents that included former and current patients. When this occurs one is very conscious, during the course of the presentation, of the process of therapy with these patients, and this awareness may result in some constraint to avoid certain topics and clinical illustrations because of the effect it might have on them.

The resident in treatment with a faculty member may be concerned that some slippage will occur and that material conveyed in a therapy hour will be utilized inadvertently in the therapist's evaluation of the resident for continuing in the residency program or for candidacy for an analytic institute. This suspicion must be considered legitimate, explored fully, and ultimately laid to rest.

CANDIDATES OF PSYCHOANALYTIC INSTITUTES

At one time only psychiatrists were accepted as candidates by most institutes. This is no longer true, and members of several disciplines in the field of mental health may now be considered for enrollment in most institutes. All recognized institutes require candidates to undergo an extensive personal analysis, called the training analysis, as part of the curriculum. Candidates are given a list of approved training analysts and must pick one acceptable to that particular institute. Usually a minimum number of hours, approximately 500–700, is required. The analysis, however, may be prolonged far beyond the minimum, when indicated. Most of the time this requirement causes no severe problem. The candidate usually picks an institute that he or she respects and looks forward, albeit ambivalently, to the experience of a training analysis with an outstanding analyst. Often he or she may be charged a reduced fee. Most of the time this arrangement works out well, and the candidate feels that he or she is getting excellent training in the field of choice. Although analysis is costly and time consuming, there is rarely any question about whether the analyst is prolonging the analysis unnecessarily.

The analyst is not only the patient's therapist but usually is also a member of the faculty of the institute and often an important figure in the psychiatric community in which the patient may want to practice. The candidate desires the approval of this analyst since it may be extremely important to his or her career. There may come a time when the candidate feels fully analyzed, but the therapist feels that the process should continue. The analysand may not feel free to speak up. By then, he or she has made a major investment in time and money, and certification by the institute is of great importance. He or she may then feel trapped and "a captive patient" until freed by the analyst. Greenson (1967) has mentioned that some of his patients, who are candidates, do not express anger or hostility to him. Instead, however, they are often very critical and hostile to other members of the institute, and/or to certain courses. This negative transference is displaced from the therapist to other targets that are not so vital to the candidate. For the analysis to proceed, the resistance to the awareness of the transference must be dealt with, and candidate and analyst must become more fully cognizant of the subject's feelings. Well-trained analysts are aware of this; when these resistances occur, they can successfully analyze them.

TRANSFERENCE AND COUNTERTRANSFERENCE

Classical analysis proceeds best when the patient knows little about the therapist as a person. The therapist is then a neutral and objective observer, and the patient can begin to express himself or herself freely, seeing the analyst as a blank screen on which to safely project feelings and thoughts. In so doing the patient can transfer past attitudes onto the person of the therapist (Little, 1981). It is also preferable for the therapist to start off knowing little about the patient so that the treatment can be conducted in the customary detached and rational manner. The therapist who is free of any preconceived ideas is more readily able to listen to the patient with nonjudgmental acceptance. Most therapists prefer to be personally anonymous to the patient, and they limit their contacts with patients to the office. Here the analyst can observe everything that goes on between them and conduct therapy in the accustomed way, sitting behind the head of the person lying outstretched on the couch. Illustrative of the patient's need to perceive the analyst as he or she wishes is an incident author Samuel Greenberg (s.G.) remembers when a patient saw him in the lobby of his office building. At the next session the patient said, "I never realized how short you were. In the office I see you as seven feet tall." Of course, this had to be analyzed at the appropriate time.

A special dilemma is posed when the analysand is a resident or colleague who has personal contact with the analyst, a fairly frequent occurence in small communities with residency training programs and a paucity of analysts not affiliated with the department. When patient and therapist are in the same field, inevitably their paths will cross. They will happen upon each other on many occasions outside the office, at conferences, seminars, lectures, parties, and concerts. There is also the likelihood that they will hear about each other through colleagues' conversation and gossip may travel far. Many therapists may prefer to be the observers and not the observed. They want to be able to control what they wish to reveal about themselves and when and to whom they choose to do this. Sometimes what the patient hears may interfere with the process of therapy. He or she may hear criticism of the "beloved" analyst at a seminar, or criticism of theories or publications. The therapist's private life may be discussed by others, and what the analysand hears may hinder the transference. Some analysts do get divorced, and some are sued by patients. They experience the gamut of difficulties that all human beings encounter. The first seminar that s.g. attended where his training analyst was serving as cochairman was somewhat disconcerting for him. For the first time, he was not listening exclusively to his analyst but to eight others as well. Also, the cochairman was not as deferential to the "great man" as s.g. thought he should have been. This had a disturbing effect on s.g. Similarly, author Florence Kaslow (f.k.) was disconcerted the first time she saw her analyst at a professional organization social event with his wife. Seeing him in his other real life-role being attentive to someone else made him seem less totally available and receptive to her.

As mentioned earlier, education and therapy overlap. A patient may, on occasion, state that he or she was "trained" by the therapist. Although we have felt satisfied with the progress and reactions of most of our therapist-patients, there are some who caused much consternation by their misrepresentation to others of our role-relationship. There was a social worker, in treatment with s.g. rather briefly, who went around broadcasting instead that she was trained by him. She did some bizarre things in therapy, but he could not set the record straight without disclosing privileged and confidential material. Quite recently f.k. had a psychiatrist enter psychoanalytically oriented treatment with her. After three sessions, he said that since he had recently begun private practice, he had no medical insurance coverage plan, but he could deduct the sessions as "educational" if he were billed for supervision. They had to deal with the role confusion, and how this would hamper the development of the transference, as well as with the ethical dilemma he was posing for both of them as he sought to manipulate the relationship for financial gain. F.K.'s refusal to accede to the request led them into his characteristic personality style of seeking to control and getting angry when anyone, especially a woman, did not acquiesce to his charmingly presented demand. Particularly in a training environment, one must be careful to keep the lines between therapy, supervision, consultation, friendship, and mentorship clear (Kaslow, 1972; Abroms, 1977). Not to do so is to confuse and render a disservice to analyst, patient, and supervisee alike. In light of all of the foregoing, it is less surprising to recall that Sigmund Freud would not accept Wilhelm Reich as a patient and that Reich harbored a great deal of resentment toward Freud for this.

When patients living in the same locale are mental health professionals, they are also colleagues and even competitors. Consider, for example, the case of a prominent analyst in New York City who was regularly upset whenever he heard that one of his former analysands was charging higher fees than he was. Many professors experience similar turmoil when former residents earn more or become more prominent than they. At one time, there was a psychiatric resident in treatment with S.G. who frequently asked to borrow books that the latter had in his office. If he were an ordinary patient S.G. would have been confident in assenting or refusing, depending on the appropriateness of the request. However, as he was a younger colleague, S.G. did lend him some books. The patient sensed the ambivalence and exploited it, keeping the books longer than he was supposed to, and returning them a little worse for wear. In time, both patient and analyst's behavior were analyzed.

SUMMARY AND FINAL COMMENTS

We have tried to cover some of the main benefits and pitfalls of treating one's colleagues. Many of them make interesting and stimulating patients; others engender feelings of uneasiness and make one feel manipulated and perhaps exploited. Unethical behavior may surface, and this invariably poses a tremendous dilemma. It needs to be dealt with as part of the behavior being analyzed. Boundary issues and the kind of therapeutic alliance that can be established in the context of an often enmeshed department of psychiatry and/or psychology have been addressed.

It seems arbitrary and often unworkable when analytic societies and institutes, particularly in small communities, forbid any contact outside the therapy hour. It is not unheard of for analyst and patient to meet unintentionally at a small dinner party and have to decide which one will leave. Everyone present is likely to figure out the relationship, so that confidentiality may be more impaired by the exit than by both remaining and keeping their contact superficial. Also, the possible rudeness to the host and hostess must be considered since therapy must be part of a real life that does not go "on hold" for the duration of the treatment process. Conversely, frequent or intense contact outside the sanctuary of the analyst's office mitigates the specialness of the treatment alliance and the benefits of classical analysis to be derived from analyzing a transference relationship. Thus it may be that didactic analyses and treatment of one's own colleagues for more distinctly therapeutic reasons is simultaneously a privilege, an honor, and a relationship fraught with potential challenges and subtle difficulties.

References

Abroms, G. M. Supervision as metatherapy. In F. W. Kaslow (Ed.), *Supervision, consultation and staff training in the helping professions*. San Francisco: Jossey Bass, 1977.

Brenner, C. *The mind in conflict*. New York: International Universities Press, 1982.

Freud, A. *The ego and the mechanisms of defense*. New York: International Universities Press, 1971 (Rev. Ed. of Writings of Anna Freud, Vol. II, 1936).

Gill, M. M. *Analysis of transference*, Vol. 1. New York: International Universities Press, 1982.

Greenson, R. R. *Technique and practice of psychoanalysis*. New York: International Universities Press, 1967.

Horney, K. *Neurosis and human growth*. New York: Norton, 1950.

Kadis, A., & Markowitz, M. Short term analytic treatment of married couples in a group by a therapist couple. In C. Sager and H. S. Kaplan (Eds.), *Progress in Group and Family Therapy*. New York: Brunner/Mazel, 1972.

Kaslow, F. W. (Ed). *Issues in human services: A sourcebook for supervision and staff development*. San Francisco: Jossey Bass, 1972.

Little, M. I. *Transference neurosis and transference psychosis*. New York: Jason Aronson, 1981.

Paolino, T. J. Some similarities and differences between psychoanalysis and psychoanalytic psychotherapy: An unsettled controversy. *Journal of Operational Psychiatry*, 1981, *12*, 105–114.

Portnoy, I. The school of Karen Horney. In S. Arieti (Ed.). *American Hand-Book of Psychiatry*, 2nd Edition. New York: Basic Books, 1974.

Waelder, R. *Basic theory of psychoanalysis*. New York: Schocken Books, 1964.

EDITOR'S COMMENTARY

When the Therapist Seeks Analysis

No doubt, in some quarters, therapists feel that unless they have been analyzed, they haven't really gone through proper therapy. This attitude is likely to be most prevalent in communities that have a large psychoanalytic cadre that promulgates this version about the best of all possible therapies. Anyone who goes into brief therapy or even longer therapies that are not psychoanalytic in nature may feel pressured about not having sufficiently restructured his or her personality or not having developed adequate insight— whatever that may constitute.

Thus, students in programs with an analytic orientation are likely to gravitate toward analysis. So, too, there are graduate therapists who feel that perhaps they have missed an essential experience or that they haven't delved sufficiently into their unconscious to be able to function at their peak ability. There continues to be a realistic attitude that psychoanalysis is the treatment of choice for certain kinds of dysfunctions and as a training technique for some therapists. There is also perhaps a glamourized image of psychoanalysis as the panacea for all. In this chapter, there is agreement with the first statement and not the second.

The cost of analysis is likely to be far greater than the cost of any other therapy. This economic issue is raised here, although it is not addressed in terms of specific figures. No price tag can be put on any therapy because there is tremendous variation in different regions and communities throughout the country and because of analysts' varying skills and reputations.

In this chapter, as in several of the others, the salient issue of dual relationships is addressed. It is important that this be considered in light of the ethical principles promulgated by some of the professions. In the American Psychological Association's 1981 revision of its Ethical Principles, Principle 6 (which deals with "welfare of the consumer") highlights a stance on this issue. It states:

> Psychologists are continually cognizant of their own needs and of their own potentially influential position vis-a-vis persons such as clients, students, and subordinates. They avoid exploiting the trust and dependency of such persons. Psychologists make every

31

effort to avoid dual relationships which could impair their professional judgment or increase the risk of exploitation. Examples of such dual relationships include but are not limited to research with and treatment of employees, students, supervisees, close friends.

Some of the chapters indicate that actual practice is somewhat different from what is espoused in this principle. We raise here the dilemma which this points to particularly in small communities where the paucity of available resources sets up the context for dual and multiple relationships. It is perhaps easiest to pick this up where there is least contradiction to the principle in psychoanalysis, where there is greatest clarity about keeping the relationship uncontaminated. Nonetheless, even here one could push it to the extreme and then find that the analyst must see therapist/patients at professional and staff meetings. One hopes that we can keep the roles separate without becoming so arbitrary that people can't even be in the same room at a professional meeting or social event to which they have both been invited without knowledge that the other would also be in attendance. More attention needs to be paid to where normal, overlapping relationships end and complex, unwise dual relationships begin so that therapists, supervisors, and professors do not find themselves inadvertently and with all good intention violating the above principle.

3

The Interface of Personal Treatment and Clinical Training for Psychotherapist Trainees

Nadine J. Kaslow, PH.D.*
Diane Friedman, PH.D.

Although it is very common for psychotherapists-in-training to obtain personal treatment during their training years, there is little exploration in the professional journals of issues related to the experiences either of being a student in concurrent training and treatment or of being the therapist of these patients. This relative gap in the literature reflects at least two factors. The first is that trainees, who tend to regard themselves as a special class of patients by virtue of the temporal contiguity of their treatment and training, publish few nonresearch articles until they achieve professional status.[1] By then, both the clarity with which they have seen and the intensity with which they have felt the interlocking effects of the treatment and training they have undergone have diminished appreciably. The second is that experienced psychotherapists simply have not tended to view patients who are psychotherapists-in-training as being either a different enough or a problematic enough subclass of patients to warrant discussion in the literature.

After reviewing the sparse existing literature that is relevant to the treatment of psychotherapist trainees as a class, we present the information we obtained and the impressions we formed from in-

---

*The order of the authors is random.

terviewing a number of clinical psychology doctoral students who were simultaneously being seen in psychotherapeutic treatment and some experienced psychologists and social workers who customarily treat such patients.[2] Although we limited our sample of students to clinical psychology doctoral candidates, we assume that most issues relevant to their training and concurrent treatment are equally germane both for master's level social work candidates and psychiatric residents. However, we do not assume great similarity between our sample and analytic candidates for two reasons. The first is that analytic training requires personal analyses of its students, whereas the more generic programs mentioned above do not. The second is that most analytic candidates have already had considerable experience as therapists prior to undertaking postgraduate work. They therefore constitute a different subclass of trainees from the more naive, less-skilled group who have a choice about entering treatment and on which we have focused our attention. Hence, we do not review in any detail the psychoanalytic literature that discusses the indispensable role of the training analysis or the realms of interplay between the training analyst, the analytic candidate, and the analytic institute. (See Chapter 2.)

Garfield and Bergin (1971) argue against ongoing personal therapy for psychotherapists-in-training. In a study they conducted, they found that trainees who had a great deal of personal treatment were able to facilitate less change in their own patients (as measured by MMPI indices) than were trainees who had had little treatment themselves. This was true despite the fact that the high-therapy trainees did not appear to be more disturbed on the MMPI (scales D, Pt, Sc) than did the low-therapy trainees. Garfield and Bergin speculate that treatment disrupts the learning process all too often by maximizing trainees' tendencies to self-absorption. As others have pointed out, these findings are consistent with Strupp's (1960) conclusions that the personal treatments of less experienced therapists tend to have either no effect or negative effects on their empathic abilities, while the personal treatments of more experienced therapists tend to enhance their sensitivity to their patients. The dominant counterargument to this point of view outside the analytic journals is voiced by Szurek and Berlin (1966). These authors take the position that personal treatment helps trainees modulate their reactions to the conflicts the training process itself stirs up in them and, as a consequence, it enhances their psychotherapeutic effectiveness.

There is considerable controversy in the literature about whether personal psychotherapy, regardless of whether it is obtained before, during, or after training, is a prerequisite for being a good therapist. Three major views have emerged (for a review see Fisher & Greenberg, 1977; Parloff, Waskow, & Wolfe, 1978). The first view is that personal therapy is either indispensable to, or very helpful in, doing effective treatment (Baum, 1973; Buckley, Karasu, & Charles, 1981; Fromm-Reichman, 1950; McNair et al., 1964; Peebles, 1980; Rubinfine, 1971; Wexler, 1971). Those who take this position cite the following expectable professional benefits: experientially derived knowledge of what it is like to be a patient, reduced tendency to develop undetected countertransference problems, enhanced listening ability as a result of freed-up defenses and increased cognitive flexibility, and more stable and elevated self-esteem. Rubinfine admits that the therapist's personal treatment can have temporary negative effects on the treatment he or she simultaneously conducts. These negative consequences arise by virtue of the overwhelming anxieties with which therapists in treatment (indeed, any patients) are sometimes flooded. Rubinfine asserts, however, that these temporary difficulties are later compensated for by the improved functioning of the therapist-patient as his or her personal treatment progresses.

The second position is that personal therapy is necessary only for some therapists at some times (Burton, 1973; Fierman, 1965; Leader, 1971). According to this view, therapists should and do enter treatment in much the same way that nonmental health professionals do: when they are feeling stressed by their personal lives and unable to cope effectively. For those individuals whose coping abilities are satisfactory, however, treatment is unnecessary (Burton, 1973; Rubinfine, 1971).

The third view is that personal psychotherapy either has limited utility for the treating therapist or is altogether unnecessary (Holt & Luborsky, 1958; Katz, Lorr, & Rubinstein, 1958; McNair, Lorr, & Callahan, 1963). In their study of psychiatric residents at the Menninger Foundation, Holt and Luborsky found no relationship at all between supervisors' ratings of residents' clinical competencies and the existence or length of residents' personal treatment histories. In commenting on this study, however, Fisher and Greenberg (1977) questioned the extent to which supervisory ratings can be regarded as valid indices of therapeutic competency *as it affects the patient*. Finally, in one study focusing on patient improvement rates (Katz, Lorr, & Rubinstein, 1958) and in another study examining premature termination rates (McNair et al., 1964), the findings were that there was a positive correlation between treatment outcome and experience level of the therapist, but not between treatment outcome and personal treatment history of the therapist.

In an effort to elucidate some of the heretofore unexplored issues related to the psychotherapy of psychotherapist trainees, we employed an open-ended, semistructured interview format in speaking with clinical psychology graduate students about their simultaneous experiences of being in training and in treatment (see Appendix 1, the "Trainee Questionnaire"). To balance our perspective, we also spoke with psychotherapists who had each treated substantial numbers of clinical psychology graduate students over the years. Here, too, we used an open-ended, semistructured interview format to elicit their thoughts about this process (see Appendix 2, the "Therapist Questionnaire"). What follows in this chapter is the description of the perspectives of the psychotherapist trainees and the experienced professionals whom we interviewed. Rather than present the specific data in detail, we have chosen to highlight some of the more prominent issues that emerged from our discussions with these individuals.

THE TRAINEES' PERSPECTIVE

Fourteen clinical psychology graduate students from six well-respected, APA-approved clinical psychology PH.D. programs in the United States were interviewed. All of these individuals were in treatment concurrently with their training. Although most claimed to be in psychodynamic psychotherapies, a few mentioned other orientations as well, notably Gestalt, eclectic, and phenomenological. The theoretical orientations of the programs these students were enrolled in spanned the continua from the cognitive-behavioral to the more traditionally psychodynamic approaches and from the more empirical to the more clinical emphases. The least advanced students were in their second year of training; the most advanced had completed internship but not the dissertation.

Of the fourteen therapists-in-training, eight had been in treatment prior to entering graduate school. Of these eight, however, six had had to terminate and then begin treatment again with new therapists in order to attend their graduate schools, which were located in other parts of the country. Of the eight trainees interviewed at or beyond internship level, five had had to terminate treatment in order to relocate to their internship sites. This striking multiplicity of moves and the consequent therapist/therapy shifts are not at all unusual among clinical psychology graduate students who live and train outside the New York City or Los Angeles areas, where clinical programs and solid internships abound. Thus, the conflict between the desire for first-rate professional training and the preference for continuous personal treatment is a common and ongoing one for many clinical trainees. Within our sample, compromise measures adopted to resolve the career-versus-therapy dilemma were as follows: preservation of treatment continuity by not moving and, instead, limiting professional options; preservation of treatment continuity by continuing with regular therapy sessions over the phone (see Chapter 9 for further description of this mode of treatment), thereby keeping professional options open; leaving therapy on a temporary basis for a year's internship and then returning; or opting from the beginning for a time-limited treatment designed to coincide with academic turning points.

By and large, the trainees who entered treatment during their training claimed to have done so for personal reasons rather than for professional ones. Most chose to go into treatment in response to the exacerbating stresses of relocating and adapting to graduate school demands. Typically, these were cited as having brought chronic problems into clear view. One individual, however, said he entered therapy primarily in response to "peer pressure." According to this trainee, who evidently felt tyrannized by the process, his classmates had refused to take him seriously as a student unless he entered treatment. It seems of some interest that although numerous psychodynamic writers have espoused the necessity of personal therapy/analysis for the conduct of effective treatment, we found little evidence that clinical psychology graduate students actually enter therapy for predominantly professional purposes.

We asked members of our trainee sample what it was that they had requested of their referral sources when seeking a therapist. We learned that until approximately the end of the second year, students' requests are not very different from those nonprofessionals make when they decide to embark upon treatment. As training progresses and naiveté decreases, however, referral requests become more pointed and tend to include specifications about the sex, theoretical orientation, personality features, and techniques of the prospective therapist.

Many of the clinical graduate students feel it is important to them that their own therapists hold PH.D.s in clinical psychology. In our sample, taking into account only the trainee's current therapist, eight trainees were in treatment with PH.D. psychologists; one with a PSY.D.; three with M.D.s; and two with M.S.W.s. However, the majority of the participants, including several in current treatment with other than PH.D. psychologists, asserted that all things being equal, they would have preferred treatment with PH.D. clinical psychologists. Trainees indicated two reasons for this preference. The first, articulated directly by almost everyone in the sample, was the wish to have a professional role model with whom to identify. The second, expressed less directly, involves an acute sensitivity to professional status issues, particularly for students in the early years of training: social workers and non-PH.D. psychologists are viewed as lower-class citizens and M.D.s are viewed as upper-class citizens.

In addition to the wish to be in therapy with PH.D. psychologists, a high percentage of the female students in our sample, frustrated by the relative scarcity of women on their graduate school faculties, expressed preferences for female therapists (by whom few of them were in fact being treated). This quest for role models in the service of constructing a sense of professional identity that we found among members of our sample has been similarly observed among psychiatric residents (Ford, 1963; Kernberg, 1968; Menninger, 1968).

As it does for most patients, the matter of psychotherapy fees poses a considerable problem for psychotherapist trainees. Some students took out loans, some borrowed from family members, some went to low-fee clinics, and some worked out special payment arrangements with their therapists (such as reduced fees or extended payment periods). Like all patients, students had a variety of reactions to therapists' reducing fees for them. The one common response that seems specific to psychotherapist trainees, however, is the sense of responsibility this arrangement has reportedly created in them to make it a practice themselves eventually to treat a number of low-fee patients (students) in the private-practice setting.

Students presented a broad range of attitudes about the often problematic borderland that lies between the domains of personal therapy and supervision. Surprisingly, some expressed the belief that clinical case discussions fall outside the realm of their personal treatments. Others, constituting the bulk of our sample, consider talk about their work, with a primary emphasis on countertransference problems, as being integral to their therapies. In the context of their personal treatment, these trainees do not seem to feel at all confused about what constitutes therapy and what constitutes supervision. The one possible exception is an individual who found it helpful to concretize the boundary between treatment and supervision by formally negotiating with her own therapist for supervision and consultation hours scheduled apart from her own therapy sessions.

In the context of their supervisory experiences, however, trainees said they have considerably more difficulty defining for themselves what the boundaries actually are or should be in the supervision relationship. The most common problem people have is in knowing "just how far to go" in discussing countertransference issues with their supervisors. This problem has been described as problematic by various authors (Campbell, 1982; Halleck & Woods, 1962). In general, the trainees expressed a preference for focusing in supervision on how to use their own countertransference reactions effectively with patients and for reserving for their personal therapies any deep scrutiny of the specific sources of their own reactions. Some trainees said that their supervisors are very helpful in teaching them to set comfortable limits for themselves in supervision; others said that their supervisors are often insensitive to their personal boundaries. In both cases, however, trainees commonly believe they are in the process of learning to take increased responsibility for setting supervision limits themselves. Interestingly, there is a greater tendency for advanced students than there is for less advanced students to regard countertransference-based supervision as a less intrusive and more helpful means of increasing therapeutic efficacy with patients. There is uniform agreement in this regard that supervisory suggestions and explanations are most needed in the early years and that supervision that is heavily countertransference-based during the first two years of clinical training serves more to confuse and create excessive anxiety in the trainee than it does to facilitate the training process.

Speaking with trainees from diverse clinical programs highlighted the reality that different clinical departments have very different collective attitudes about the necessity for and/or desirability
of their students' being in treatment. At one extreme is a department that, reportedly, overtly ignores the whole issue but covertly
conveys the notion that a student's need to be in treatment reflects
negatively on the department's ability to choose emotionally stable, hence adequate, graduate students. In this program and others with similar leanings, peer support in the form of a pro-treat-
ment attitude typically emerges. In addition, nonuniversity-based
supervisors play a more active role in encouraging students to seek
treatment and helping them find appropriate therapists. At the
other extreme is a department that actively encourages all students
to enter therapy. In this situation and those that approximate it,
student collusion with the faculty point of view seems normative.
The outcome is peer pressure on resistant classmates to enter treatment. Apparently, a number of programs that do encourage students to embark upon personal therapy facilitate the process by lo-
cating experienced, but low-fee, clinicians for them.

A surprisingly large number of trainees ($N = 7$) reported seeing therapists who are affiliated in some capacity with the clinical
psychology programs at their respective universities. The personal
interrelationships underlying the resultant treatment situations are
so complex that they defy clear categorization. Within our sample,
one of the easier situations to describe is as follows: Trainee A is in
treatment with Therapist B. B is a good friend of A's clinical supervisors, socializes with and is on the doctoral committees of A's peers,
and, finally, is on the internship admissions committee at the site
to which A has applied. Again, this is one of the *least* complex of
the treatment relationships we discovered.

Some students stated that their therapists' outside knowledge
of significant people in the trainee's world facilitates the treatment
process. They believe that the therapist's capacity to help them reality test more than compensates for the loss of privacy that they
experience. Others, however, feel seriously inhibited by the various loyalty conflicts that are thereby activated within treatment.
These conflicts are felt to be particularly problematic when the not
uncommon circumstance arises in which the trainee has negative
reactions to someone known to be the friend, colleague, student,
or therapist of the trainee's therapist. Although a number of trainees seemed to sense intuitively that their own negative reactions to

people in the therapist's professional and social sphere are, at least in part, manifestations of transference phenomena, they complained that the blurred boundaries between their own and their therapists' worlds render these phenomena awkward and intractable.

Additionally, a number of students complained of problems they have in dealing with the multiple forms of unsolicited information about their therapist that they receive from faculty (in the classroom), supervisors, and classmates. Often, putting a stop to this flow of information requires stating openly that one is in an ongoing or past treatment relationship with a particular therapist. This is experienced by the trainees as a violation of their right to privacy.

Students also stated that peer relations are often negatively affected when classmates are in treatment with, being supervised by, or are friends of a given trainee's own therapist. Although only some students articulated the value of dealing openly with these issues in treatment and with their friends, a large number expressed irritation with the additional pressures that being part of the therapist's professional and social communities imposes upon them.

The extent to which trainees are preoccupied with questions concerning their own diagnoses very much reflects the diversity of attitudes within the field of psychology itself about the value and meaning of diagnosis. There seems to be a trend for students from predominantly empirical and cognitive-behavioral programs to be less concerned about such questions than are their counterparts from predominantly applied and psychodynamic programs. Those who are most caught up in the medical school syndrome ("You name it, I've got it") expressed considerable anxiety about being "found out" and, as a consequence, asked to leave their programs. Of these, a number claimed to have eventually taken heart from their evolving recognition that select faculty members carry diagnoses either similar to or "worse than" their own. Among this group, the most commonly voiced concern is the fear of being "borderline."

Trainees enumerated several ways in which they feel their personal treatments are (or had been) impacting positively on their clinical work. The first is in the growth of their own respect for the struggles their patients have in therapy. The second is in the diminished need to "do for" patients and the simultaneously enhanced ability to "be with" them instead. The third is in an increased capacity to differentiate their own affective states from those of their patients. The fourth is in the development of a more realistic time perspective in relation to treatment processes and goals. And the fifth is in the growth of the capacity to attend to untoward countertransference reactions.

In reciprocal fashion, the trainees also believe that their clinical training experiences promote growth in and of themselves, and that, further, they increase both a trainee's responsivity to and investment in his or her personal treatment. On the whole, they seem to feel that their academic courses, outside readings, clinical practice, and supervision all serve to increase their openness to scrutinizing transference manifestations in their personal therapies. Equally, they are grateful for the self-discoveries that have been prompted by exploration of their countertransference reactions to patients. In particular, a number of trainees referred to the unexpected unearthing of their own rescue fantasies. In another vein, they mentioned the increasingly accurate perspectives they believe they are developing regarding their own pathology by virtue of observations drawn from their own patient contacts. And, finally, several trainees who described themselves as being characterologically "too tight" and "overcontrolled" expressed gratitude toward their more relaxed patients, whose examples of "being" in treatment serve as models for them in their personal therapies.

Trainees are equally aware of negative effects on their clinical work as a result of being in concurrent training and treatment. Overidentification with the patient role was cited as a problem. Also mentioned was despair regarding the efficacy of clinical work at times when the trainee feels at an impasse in his or her personal therapy. More commonly, however, students spoke of the problem of their own flooding affects, newly freed up in treatment, which reduce their capacity to think clearly and attend well to their patients. A number reported overwhelming stress from having, as a consequence, to invent facades of competency and adequacy in order to manage the work with their patients. The problem seems simply to be that having to perform a function one has not yet learned at the same time that one is existing in the graduate school environment (described variously by members of our sample as "paranoia inducing," "regression promoting," and "like a year-long IQ test") *and* undergoing the affectively stimulating experience of personal treatment, is often "just too much."

Trainees commonly referred to complications in their personal therapies that they feel are brought about by their trainee status. They pointed to their own heightened tendencies to intellectualize as being, at least in part, a function of having access to a great deal of technical information. In addition, knowledge about regression derived from clinical training activities seems to create pressure on many students involved in psychodynamic treatments to "be good patients" by regressing "appropriately." Conversely, a number of trainees in relatively nonpsychodynamic treatments and training programs reported the fear that any recognizable regression implies incipient psychosis. It may well be that regression-anxious trainees preselect nondynamic forms of treatment and training and that regression-eager trainees steer themselves into more dynamic treatment situations and programs. Nevertheless, the point seems worth making that the training students receive in their clinical programs about what is and is not expected, useful, and interesting in patients is perceived as influencing the way trainees conduct themselves in their own personal treatment, at least during the first year.

Furthermore, a preponderance of the sample reported feelings of inhibition at some point in their personal treatment about describing to their therapists their work with their own patients. The assumption made is that the therapist, an experienced worker in the same profession as the trainee-patient, will be more acutely aware and critical of the trainee's errors than would someone who is in a different field. Most students, however, reported that their anxieties about discussing their professional work in treatment abate in inverse proportion to the growth of their feelings of competency and professional rootedness.

Another complication cited by trainees involves manifestations of their struggles with differentiation rather than with competency issues. Students mentioned inhibitions about openly describing or discussing with their therapists those areas of their professional lives about which they and their therapists presumably differ. These areas typically include trainees' theoretical orientation, therapeutic techniques and personal style, and career goals.

In an effort to gauge the extent to which trainees view their personal therapies as an overall asset in the training experience, we asked students to rank-order the educative value of the following: outside readings, academic coursework, clinical practice, supervision, and personal treatment. Only one student ranked "readings" at the top of the list. The others, regardless of number of years of training, ranked clinical practice, personal treatment, and supervision, in descending order, as having had (or having) the most impact on them as clinicians.

THE THERAPISTS' PERSPECTIVE

The eight psychotherapists with whom we spoke ranged in experience from seven to thirty years, post degree. A number of them indicated that their caseloads are composed primarily of mental health professionals, including clinical psychology trainees. Most of the therapists we interviewed are psychodynamic in orientation, but one or two described themselves as having an essentially phenomenological slant.

Commonly, the therapists denied at the outset of the interviews that they see psychotherapist-trainees as a distinct class of patients. However, it became evident as they talked and thought about the issue more that this is not the case. Most of the therapists soon recognized that there are either characteristics of trainees or features of the treatment of this group of patients about which it is possible for them to generalize. In addition, some came to realize that they have long been in the habit of making such generalizations about this group.

There was consensus that, like many non-mental health professionals and most experienced psychotherapists, clinical psychology trainees fall in the category of the motivated and psychologically minded YAVIS (young, attractive, verbal, intelligent, successful) patient. Some therapists, however, who treat large numbers of graduate students from cognitive-behavioral and/or empirical programs, said they find the sophistication levels regarding dynamic concepts (in particular, transference, somatization, the value of dreams) to be so low among such students that they exclude these trainee-patients from the category into which they place students from more dynamically oriented programs.

The latter observation provokes questions about why it is that trainees with cognitive-behavioral orientations would seek treatment from psychodynamic therapists in the first place. At least part of the answer seems to lie in the reality that the more classically cognitive-behavioral clinicians, at least in the communities from which we drew our sample, work professionally in academic rather than clinical sectors. They are therefore unavailable to students as potential treatment agents. Those practicing psychotherapists who do employ cognitive-behavioral treatment techniques tend to do so within the context of more psychodynamic relationship-oriented frameworks.

Approximately half of our sample stated the belief that there is no normative diagnosis among clinical psychology trainees. Many of the therapists did refer to the superficial obsessional defenses that clinical trainees typically manifest early in treatment, but none described trainees as being preponderantly obsessional in the classical sense. However, almost half of our sample did suggest that there is a greater tendency for such students to be borderline narcissistic characters than there is for members of the general population to be. Several therapists who expressed this belief pointed to the selection standards of clinical programs as being responsible for the situation. The unusually high standards of achievement by which clinical admissions committees rate their applicants (made possible by the very large numbers of applicants to the top programs, which accept very small classes) has led to the eventual acceptance into the field of a high percentage of students whose superior cognitive development is just the visible flag for what one therapist in our sample termed the "superb" false self constructions (Winnicott, 1965) of many clinical students. Some therapists further stated that not only do trainees tend, as a rule, to have more "primitive" internal structures than people in the general population, but they also tend to be psychologically less intact than most professional therapists who are seen in treatment. The reason offered to account for this phenomenon is that experienced therapists, by virtue of age alone, have had more years of productive personal therapy than trainees have had and are, therefore, a higher-functioning group.

However, a number of therapists with whom we spoke were of the opinion that it is easier to treat trainees than more experienced psychotherapists. They see trainees as less difficult to work with owing to the following three factors: their enthusiasm for and hopeful attitude toward the change process, their relatively less rigid character defenses (as a function of their youth), and their less fixed identifications with the role of "healer."

Other differences between trainee-patients and therapist-patients were noted. One hinges on the fact that, as a group, trainees tend to be in their mid- to late twenties, whereas practicing professionals are generally older. As a consequence, identity issues are typically more salient for the student group than for the professional group. Another difference is in the nature of the impetus that prompts both trainees and professionals to question whether or not they are in the right field. Usually, students worry that they are "too crazy" or not bright enough to be effective psychotherapists. Many who explore their motives for choosing to become therapists while they are still in training develop concerns about the neurotic nature of that choice. In contrast, experienced therapists tend to question the rightness of their professional choice in response to the combined effects of mid-life crises and the burnout syndromes that overwhelm them. Most often, members of the latter group complain of the daily isolation from peers, the perpetual need to maintain careful control of their emotions, the heightened awareness of their own personal problems, the frustrated omnipotence wishes, the relentless ambiguity of the treatments they conduct, the lack of immediate gratification in their work, and the overexposure to both depressed and borderline patients (Bermak, 1977; Chessick, 1978; Fine, 1980).

Although the literature suggests that there is a range of attitudes regarding the value of personal psychotherapy for psychotherapists, there was unanimous agreement among members of our sample that personal treatment is integral to the training of mental health professionals. There was also agreement that the therapist plays many roles in relation to his or her trainee-patients, including those of supervisor, teacher, and role model. Most of the therapists said they offer occasional didactic explanations to their trainee-patients and also provide some form of supervision for them from time to time. Only one therapist said that he does not engage in anything that resembles supervision. In this particular case, the therapist, whose various activities in the training community include the assignment of trainees to supervisors at a major training site, scrupulously avoids providing trainee-patients with supervision in the treatment context in deference to his supervisory staff, whose authority he does not want to undermine.

Oddly, almost all of the other therapists we interviewed hastened to assure us that they regard "too many" requests for supervision during treatment as a sign of "resistance" from the patient. This assurance was offered so spontaneously and with such regularity that we can only assume that therapists are commonly defensive about this point. In only a single case did a therapist in our sample directly articulate her concern that her willingness to provide some form of supervision to her patients might be symptomatic of her own untoward countertransference problems.

There was a moderate degree of agreement among the therapists with whom we spoke that aspects of the training milieu place inordinate stress on students. There was, however, little agreement about what the source of the stress actually is. Some therapists stated that they see the continual direct scrutiny and evaluation of students' work during the early years of training as responsible for the high degree of chaos their trainee-patients typically evince. One said he believes that it is not so much the supervision and evaluation processes but the intensely charged nature of peer group interactions that sustains the competitive frenzy often noted among clinical students (for example, vying for "favorite child" status, "gifted" status, "most likely to succeed" status). Still another said he sees the sheer length of the training programs as being problematic by virtue of the dependency and sibling conflicts that are kept prominent for so many years. This therapist stated that, in his opinion, clinical students stay in the grips of transference longer than other patients because the training programs elicit and then sustain interminably so many areas of conflict.

Although there was no agreement among the therapists about what in the training milieu is so disruptive for clinical students, there was consensus that feelings of immobility and manifestations of generalized defensiveness are common trainee responses to the pressures of clinical graduate programs. The therapists were also uniform in their perceptions that as students increasingly develop feelings of competency about their work, the immobility and defensiveness lessen.

Therapists said they believe that the training programs have both positive and negative impact on students' personal therapies. One dynamically oriented therapist claimed that the regressions prompted by the clinical training environment increase the probability that trainee-patients will have to confront in treatment their feelings about authority figures, sibling relationships, and dependency/autonomy issues. Another therapist, in contrast, sees the uncontrolled nature of the graduate school regression as requiring him to provide a considerable amount of containment and to engage in other ego-supportive work with his trainee-patients.

This same therapist, who treats numerous students from a clinical program that stresses an object relations point of view, spoke of a phenomenon he has often encountered among such students. Reportedly, course work exposure to Guntrip (1969) and Balint (1958; 1979), among others, often leads students to become enamored of the notion of "regression as 'cure'." As a consequence, the wish to regress in an effort to achieve a magical sense of wholeness and newness is intensified in these students. The treatment implication is that this therapist, who happens to be object relational in orientation himself, finds it necessary to take a protectively antiregressive stance in these cases in order to counteract the potentially hazardous pulls of the training.

Several therapists were of the opinion that clinical programs provide optimal backdrops before which trainees can play out their developmentally appropriate separation-individuation dramas. Inevitably, people new to a field bring with them idealized conceptions of the profession they are entering and, equally inevitably, grow disillusioned as the realities of the situation intrude. As Flamm (1971) has noted, the disillusionment and mourning processes often visible in trainees through their fluctuating states of anger at and emotional withdrawal from their programs are natural manifestations of separation/individuation phenomena (Mahler, Pine, & Bergman, 1975).

Some therapists, however, stated that the clinical programs their patients attend are disruptive forces in the treatment as a result of the premature autonomy or false self functioning that training tends to promote. As the trainees in our sample pointed out, clinical students must defensively adopt facades of self-assured and competent functioning when they begin treating patients prior to having amassed more than the most rudimentary skills and knowledge required for the task. For those therapists who view the gradual unmasking of the false self defense as integral to treatment, this aspect of mental health training clearly runs counter to treatment goals.

There are numerous ways in which therapists share trainees' concerns about unclear treatment boundaries. There was uniform agreement among the therapists, however, that the task of managing those boundaries is their own. Boundary issues mentioned differed from therapist to therapist, as did the decisions about how to handle them. Among the more common professional questions raised were the following: whether or not to write letters of recommendation for patients who have also been students or supervisees of the therapist, whether or not to supervise someone who had previously been one's patient, whether or not to interrupt the treatment of a trainee whose program requires a course taught by the therapist, and whether and how to withdraw tactfully from decision-making capacities on admissions or evaluations committees without violating the trainee's right to confidentiality regarding the fact of his or her treatment.

During their early graduate school years, trainees are frequently concerned that they will be found unfit for the field by their therapists, who they fear will report this news to the training and/or professional communities. Practically speaking, however, no therapist with whom we spoke admitted to having ever considered doing so. Two of the more experienced therapists in our sample independently shared their observations that such a practice is unnecessary. In their view, a process akin to that of natural selection typically occurs in clinical training programs; trainees who seem the least well suited for the field eventually recognize this themselves and opt to avoid clinical practice.

It was apparent from talking with the therapists that there are common countertransference-provoking situations that arise with some frequency when they are treating trainees. One group of such issues concerns the therapist's colleagues who also have some sphere of interaction with the trainee-patient. Since it not infrequently happens that trainees speak unfavorably about authority figures in the professional world, therapists reported that they sometimes find themselves feeling identified with the colleague and therefore counterattack via silent (or not so silent) denigrations of the patient's judgment and perceptiveness. Equally often, the countertransference is rooted in identification with the student and is manifested by the therapist's too-hearty appreciation of the patient's anger at reportedly poor supervision or unfair academic practices. Similarly, when it occurs that the patient speaks highly of and/or idealizes a colleague of the therapist's, it is not unusual for the therapist either to feel competitive with or to identify with the valued supervisor/academician. These kinds of reactions are certainly commonplace in any treatment; the point here is that because the training and treatment worlds often overlap so extensively, especially in small communities, the situations arise more frequently and therefore have more palpable potential consequences in the treatment of trainees. All of the therapists with whom we spoke, however, noted that these problems seem to dissipate as their experience in working with this group of patients increases.

A number of the therapists described occasional untoward feelings of competitiveness with their trainee-patients. Envy of the patient's youth and excitement about the profession are not uncommon when the novelty of and illusions about the field have long since diminished for the therapist. In addition, a number mentioned their envy of the diverse and easily accessible learning opportunities available to their trainee-patients. Still others referred to competitive feelings when listening to a patient describe a particularly well-handled case.

Countertransference problems that originate outside the consulting office were also discussed by a few therapists. Some acknowledged feeling quite uncomfortable when they learn that a trainee-patient has indulged in a character assassination of the therapist while speaking with either a colleague, student, patient, or social acquaintance of the therapist. Most acutely painful are the instances in which trainee-patients do so without informing the listener that the object of the vilification is someone with whom the trainee happens to be in treatment. Somewhat less often, it happens that the therapist is present when colleagues or friends discuss a patient negatively from the point of view of a social or training context. A few of the therapists with whom we spoke admitted to boundary lapses of their own that prompt them to feel personally attacked as a consequence of such discussions.

A large proportion of our therapist sample admitted feeling a greater impulsion to monitor countertransferences with trainees and experienced psychotherapists because of how much they and the patients have in common by virtue of shared professional interests and forms of livelihood. One therapist spoke of the enhanced sense of pride and specialness she feels when working with trainees because such treatments increase her awareness that she herself has chosen a craft that requires personal transmission. Several mentioned the narcissistic gratification they experience upon getting referrals from colleagues in the academic setting. The wish to be part of the training of new therapists apparently culminates in covert status issues related to being the therapist of trainess. On the basis of the remarks of our sample, it appears that the prestige associated with being known in the community as a therapist who treats trainees approaches that associated with being known as a "therapist's therapist."

COMMENTS

In the course of gathering the data on which this chapter is based, we became increasingly intrigued by the difference of opinion between the trainees and the therapists regarding the following question: are psychotherapist-trainees a unique subgroup of patients? It will be recalled that although trainees responded "yes" to this question, most of the therapists initially responded "no." (It is, perhaps, revealing that members of the latter group were nevertheless quite willing to be interviewed about the subject.)

As we collated our interview material, it became evident that the trainees and therapists are not actually as divergent in their thinking as it had originally seemed that they were. Trainees and therapists in our sample agree that personal treatment is a necessary and integral part of the training process for mental health practitioners. Neither group asserts that the personal dynamic issues of trainees are any different from those found among members of other patient groups such as other graduate/professional students or any bright patients embarking upon new careers. But trainees and therapists do believe that the interrelatedness of trainees' professional training and personal psychotherapy experiences lends a distinctive character to their treatments. On the basis of the data we collected, the most visible distinctive features are these: the expanded range of the therapist's functions, including dispensing professional advice and serving as a professional role model; the shared personal and professional communities of therapist and patient, replete with sensitive boundary problems; and the nature and frequency of the therapist's countertransference reactions.

Trainees and therapists also tend to agree that the training in which the student is engaged is, in the long run, a growth-promoting process in and of itself. The consensus that emerged from our interviews supports Ford's (1963, p. 476) notion that the "developing psychotherapist acquires large portions of his own personal identity and self-concept collaterally with his acquisition of professional and therapeutic role and identity." In short, clinical training

and psychotherapeutic treatment work simultaneously to stimulate the progress of students' internal development.

There was also agreement among students and therapists that
clinical training is a highly stressful process that can have significant negative impact on the immediate emotional functioning of
students. This point of view has previously been expressed by
Campbell (1982, p. 1405), who regards the stresses inherent in clinical training as having the "potential for exacerbating or reactivat-
ing latent conflict" in students, thereby "contributing to the development of overt psychopathology." Although this is evidently a
painful situation for trainees, there are nevertheless some potentially positive corollaries that flow from it. The first is that students'
conflict areas are brought more sharply into focus by the clinicial
training and may therefore be more accessible because they
emerge in such an ego dystonic fashion. The second is that the personal therapies to which students tend to turn for help eventually
facilitate their gaining greater knowledge and control of themselves and, as a result, increasing their interpersonal effectiveness
with patients, faculty, family, and friends.

There is one point, however, about which trainees and therapists strongly disagree. Trainees expressed the belief that their
knowledge of psychological processes (e.g., transference, resistance, regression) renders them, almost by definition, more interesting or less resistant patients than most. The therapists, in contrast, do not see trainees as having a particularly sophisticated
knowledge base and, further, believe that some of the knowledge
they do have serves more to impede treatment (via resistance) than
promote it.

Why trainees base their assumption of specialness on the erro-
neous belief that they are highly informed about matters of pathology and treatment is not difficult to understand. As a group, clinical students typically have extensive histories of being labeled
"special" by virtue of their superior cognitive abilities and capacities to outperform others in a wide variety of life situations. That
their narcissism should find an unrestrained focus on their cognitive skills is more or less in synchrony with some of the reality features of their collective histories. It is also mild evidence in support
of the opinions of those therapists in our sample who view clinical
trainees as being a relatively narcissistic group.

Given that our data lend support to the idea that there are, indeed, some distinctive features of the therapies of clinical trainees

(perhaps the least of which is trainees' technical knowledge of the field), a more provocative question to ask is why therapists are so reluctant to acknowledge this fact either to themselves or to others. One rather bland hypothesis is that for the most part, clinicians think predominantly in diagnostic categories and are therefore unaccustomed to organizing their thoughts along the lines of occupational groups. But it has also occurred to us that the narcissism of the therapists themselves and the defenses they have erected against it are to some extent responsible for their immediate rejection of the idea that clinical trainees comprise a particular (that is, "special") subgroup of psychotherapy patients. Specific features of the treatment of trainees that exert a narcissistic pull on therapists include the following: therapist identification with trainee-patients who view themselves as "special," implicit and discomforting status issues prevalent in the professional community related to who conducts the treatment of other professionals (both experienced and inexperienced), and power and status needs of therapists that are met through their association with the academic community or by signs of approval from it via referrals. It appears that the dominant way in which therapists deal with these sensitive matters is by outright denial that trainees are "special" enough to warrant subgroup status at all. This denial then facilitates therapists' disavowal of their own feelings of specialness.

While this chapter was still in preparation we received information from a number of people we had interviewed regarding some of the consequences the interviews themselves had had for them. Numerous trainees reported that afterward they were able to bring material into their personal treatments that they had not previously presented. They felt that the legitimation of their perspectives on concurrent personal treatment and training freed them to explore some of their own related issues in more depth with their therapists. Simultaneously, a number of therapists reported afterward that thinking about these issues had increased their sensitivity to the complex nature of the interactions they have with their trainee-patients. It therefore seems clear to us that further publications about the training and personal therapy interface would be welcomed by experienced and inexperienced psychotherapists alike.

Similarly, it appears that it would be equally helpful to have access to more information about the transition phase trainees in treatment undergo as they emerge from trainee standing to full professional status. Just as the training/treatment processes largely promote individuation phenomena, the eventual emergence into professional adult status signals and entails reunion, albeit on a new footing, with the parent community from which the ex-trainee is presumably now more clearly differentiated. We wonder about the impact of this professional transition on the ongoing personal treatment of therapists, and look forward to seeing descriptions and examinations of this process in print.

References

Balint, M. The concept of subject and object in psychoanalysis. *British Journal of Medical Psychology*, 1958, *31*, 83–91.

Balint, M. *The basic fault.* London: Tavistock Publications, 1969. (Reprinted as *The basic fault.* New York: Brunner/Mazel, 1979.)

Baum, O. E. Further thoughts on countertransference. *Psychoanalytic Review*, 1973, *60*, 127–140.

Bermak, G. E. Do psychiatrists have special emotional problems? *American Journal of Psychoanalysis*, 1977, *37*, 141–146.

Buckley, P., Karasu, T. B., & Charles, E. Psychotherapists view their personal therapy. *Psychotherapy: Theory, Research, and Practice*, 1981, *18*, 299–305.

Burton, A. The psychotherapist as client. *American Journal of Psychoanalysis*, 1973, *33*, 94–103.

Campbell, H. D. The prevalence and ramifications of psychopathology in psychiatric residents: An overview. *American Journal of Psychiatry*, 1982, *139*, 1405–1411.

Chessick, R. D. The sad soul of the psychiatrist. *Bulletin of the Menninger Clinic*, 1978, *42*, 1–9.

Fierman, L. B. Myths in the practice of psychotherapy. *Archives of General Psychiatry*, 1965, *12*, 408–414.

Fine, H. Despair and depletion in the therapist. *Psychotherapy: Theory, Research, and Practice*, 1980, *17*, 392–395.

Fisher, S., & Greenberg, R. P. *The scientific credibility of Freud's theory and therapy.* New York: Basic Books, 1977.

Flamm, G. H. Discussion. *American Journal of Psychiatry*, 1971, *128*, 83–84.

Ford, E. Being and becoming a psychotherapist: The search for identity. *American Journal of Psychotherapy*, 1963, *17*, 472–482.

Fromm-Reichmann, F. *Principles of intensive psychotherapy.* Chicago: University of Chicago Press, 1950.

Garfield, S. L., & Bergin, A. E. Personal therapy, outcome, and some therapist variables. *Psychotherapy: Theory, Research, and Practice*, 1971, *8*, 251–253.

Guntrip, H. *Schizoid phenomena, object-relations and the self.* New York: International Universities Press, 1969.

Halleck, S., & Woods, S. Emotional problems of psychiatric residents. *Psychiatry*, 1962, *25*, 339–346.

Holt, R. R., & Luborsky, L. *Personality patterns of psychiatrists.* (Vol. 1). New York: Basic Books, 1958.

Katz, M. M., Lorr, M., & Rubinstein, E. A. Remainer patient attributes and their relation to subsequent improvement in psychotherapy. *Journal of Consulting Psychology*, 1958, *22*, 411–414.

Kernberg, O. Some effects of social pressure on the psychiatrist as a clinician. *Bulletin of the Menninger Clinic*, 1968, *32*, 144–159.

Leader, A. The argument against personal analysis in training for psychotherapy. In R. R. Holt (Ed.), *New horizon for psychotherapy: Autonomy as a profession*. New York: International Universities Press, 1971.

Mahler, M., Pine, F., & Bergman, A. *The psychological birth of the human infant*. New York: Basic Books, 1975.

McNair, D. M., Lorr, M., & Callahan, D. M. Patient and therapist influences on quitting psychotherapy. *Journal of Consulting Psychology*, 1963, *27*, 10–17.

McNair, D. M., Lorr, M., Young, H. H., Roth, I., & Boyd, R. W. A three-year follow-up of psychotherapy patients. *Journal of Clinical Psychology*, 1964, *20*, 258–264.

Menninger, R. The psychiatrist's identity: Quo vadis? *Bulletin of the Menninger Clinic*, 1968, *32*, 139–143.

Parloff, M. B., Waskow, I. E., & Wolfe, B. E. Research on therapist variables in relation to process and outcome. In S. L. Garfield & A. E. Bergin (Eds.), *Handbook of psychotherapy and behavior change: An empirical analysis* (Second edition). New York: John Wiley & Sons, 1978.

Peebles, M. J. Personal therapy and ability to display empathy, warmth, and genuineness in psychotherapy. *Psychotherapy: Theory, Research, and Practice*, 1980, *17*, 258–262.

Rubinfine, D. L. The role of personal psychotherapy in the training of psychotherapists. In R. R. Holt (Ed.), *New horizon for psychotherapy: Autonomy as a profession*. New York: International Universities Press, 1971.

Strupp, H. H. Nature of psychotherapists' contribution to treatment process. *Archives of General Psychiatry*, 1960, *3*, 219–231.

Szurek, S., & Berlin, I. The question of therapy for the trainee in the psychiatric training program. *Journal of the American Academy of Child Psychiatry*, 1966, *5*, 155–165.

Wexler, M. Psychoanalysis as the basis for psychotherapeutic training. In R. R. Holt (Ed.), *New horizon for psychotherapy: Autonomy as a profession*. New York: International Universities Press, 1971.

Winnicott, D. W. *The maturational processes and the facilitating environment*. New York: International Universities Press, 1965.

Notes

1. This chapter was written when one of the authors (N.K.) was still in graduate school and the other (D.F.) had just been granted her degree.
2. We wish to thank the trainees and therapists who participated in this study. For reasons of confidentiality, they must remain anonymous.

APPENDIX 1
TRAINEE QUESTIONNAIRE

1. When, why, and with whom did you enter treatment (treatment history)? How did this arrangement come about (e.g., referral source, referral request)? How are fees handled?
2. Discuss the boundary problems associated with being a trainee in treatment (e.g., supervision versus therapy, overlapping professional and social communities).
3. What are the reciprocal effects of the treatment and the training processes (e.g., effects on: development of your theoretical orientation, your functioning as a therapist/supervisee, your functioning as a patient)?
4. Rank in order of importance how each affected your clinical work: personal therapy, supervision, reading, coursework, clinical experience.

APPENDIX 2
THERAPIST QUESTIONNAIRE

1. Are psychology trainees a definable group and, if so, what defines them (e.g., personal characteristics, diagnoses)? How do they differ from the general population? How do they differ from experienced therapists?
2. Is psychotherapy an integral component of the training process? What does this imply about your role as therapist?
3. What is the impact of the patient's training on the psychotherapy process (e.g., student's knowledge of regression, affective impact of university setting)? How does this influence your behavior?
4. Discuss the boundary problems associated with your trainee patient's treatment (e.g., supervisory issues, overlapping professional and social communities). What kinds of management techniques have you adopted to deal with these? What kinds of countertransference manifestations do you typically encounter?

EDITOR'S COMMENTARY

The Flip Side of the Coin—
The Freshness of Students'
Perceptions

In attempting to put together a collection of analytic, insightful papers about why, how, and from whom therapists themselves seek treatment, it seemed that a possibly productive route of inquiry was to request an article from several students about to complete their graduate-professional training. The quest for an innovative response to these queries came to fruition in this chapter by N. Kaslow and Friedman. Judiciously, they drew up and administered an open-ended questionnaire so that their ideas and interpretations would be grounded in data acquired through a base of thoughts and perceptions broader than their own. They interviewed students and interns as well as practicing clinicians to ascertain viewpoints from patient and therapist alike.

What emerges here is the centrality of concerns over boundaries—what they are and what they should be—particularly when this special patient/therapist dyad is involved in one or more other intertwined roles such as student/teacher or research assistant/mentor. In addition, sometimes the trainee raises questions about his or her own work as a fledgling therapist and receives quasi–supervision from the senior therapist. N. Kaslow and Friedman elucidate some of the same dilemmas that Lazarus and Fay do and seem to report similar resolution, that is, rarely are the roles kept "pure." Apparently, in small communities and/or in close-knit graduate and medical school environments there may not be enough well-trained mental health professionals available to avoid these overlapping roles. What a different scene than in large metropolitan areas like New York, Chicago, Philadelphia, and Boston, where analytic institutes, psychiatric residency programs, psychology, marriage and family therapy, and social work graduate programs can insist that students be treated by someone outside the faculty and supervisory staff, because there are hundreds of licensed and respected therapists nearby. Perhaps we can no longer expect guidelines formulated in and for huge urban communities to be adhered to as rigidly in smaller towns and suburban settings where they are inapplicable.

These two incisive young women show logically that therapy trainees constitute a special subset of the therapy population and exhibit some specific differences from nontherapist patients. Although initially some of the psychotherapists interviewed negated the validity of this assumption, as they gave the matter more concentrated attention, many agreed. N. Kaslow and Friedman's hypothesis about this concurred with what J. Coché found in her group therapy with therapist-patients—that they do indeed constitute a special population, with an additional propensity for utilizing the therapist as a professional role model and for trying to extrapolate substantive theoretical material and therapeutic skill from their personal treatment experience. It may be that much of the field, of varied persuasions, has come full cycle, with trainees and young therapists spontaneously seeking something akin to the didactic (content inclusive) analysis (discussed in Chapter 2) long held to be an essential, vital part of the making of the analyst.

With sparkling vision, these authors tell us what they and their young colleagues seek and treasure in their therapists, thereby providing an antidote to the overvaluing of the more jaded, who coast on their laurels, expecting others to revere them because of their prestige and not their current therapeutic performances.

4

Hypnotherapy with Psychotherapists—An "Innocuous" Means of Seeking Help

John E. Churchill, M.S.W.

In this chapter, hypnotherapy denotes the clinical use of hypnosis in the treatment of both physical and emotional problems of psychotherapists. Hypnosis is not practiced in a vacuum, but is used as an adjunctive measure to traditional medical and psychotherapeutic procedures. While treating other therapists, I prefer to combine hypnosis with certain behavioral modification and stress management techniques to help them further balance their lives. Such a combination is not uncommon, and is usually quite viable and effective. This process is explicated later in the chapter. I find the major medical center an ideal environment for employing hypnotherapy to treat a multiplicity of physical and emotional difficulties. Such an approach can afford psychotherapists a discreet yet liberal fashion of treatment, even in their own backyard. Pain and stress management, habit problems, and arousal control to enhance performance are among the most common issues addressed.

CREDENTIALS IN THE FIELD

With referrals coming from virtually every department in the hospital, the professional hypnotherapist must be adequately and thoroughly trained. In addition, he or she must have the proper credentials to teach and supervise other professionals within the medical setting. The hypnoclinician should be a member of one of two nationally recognized societies. They are the Society for Clinical and Experimental Hypnosis (SCEH) and the American Society of Clinical Hypnosis (ASCH). SCEH requires its members to have a doctorate in medicine, dentistry, osteopathy, or psychology or to possess a master's degree in social work with affiliation in one of two national clinical registries. Members must also have completed acceptable courses in hypnotic techniques and be actively practicing hypnosis in their respective settings. Certification of competence for membership must be corroborated by two sponsors who are professionals in the field and are familiar with the skills of the applicant. I belong to SCEH, which encourages its members to publish scientific articles in hypnosis as well as to teach it in a recognized medical facility.

OVERVIEW AND CLARIFICATION

The history of hypnotherapy has been fully covered by early noted writers including Cutten (1911), Wolberg (1951), Bromberg (1954), Bramwell (1956), Conn (1958), and Rosen (1959). Contemporary authorities who have given detailed accounts of the history of clinical hypnosis include Kroger (1963, 1967), Crasilneck and Hall (1975), Spiegel (1978), and Edelstein (1981).

I have chosen to exclude a descriptive report on the various forms of individual hypnotherapy. Instead I refer to the elaborate and excellent work by Kroger (1963, 1967) in which he aptly describes these different areas. In a series of papers, Greenberg (1977) traces the development of group hypnotherapy. He also examines specific techniques when combining hypnosis with traditional group therapy modes.

In the field of hypnotherapy there are innumerable definitions of hypnosis with emphasis primarily on altered states of consciousness and misdirection of attention. I prefer the view espoused by Kline (1963), who describes it as both a state and a relationship. As a state, it possesses the characteristics of suggestibility, altered perception, availability of unconscious material, and increased awareness and sensitivity. As a relationship, hypnosis often facilitates therapy by intensifying the transference process.

Erickson, Rossi, and Rossi (1976) state that hypnotherapists share many common ideas with other psychotherapists. He emphasizes an understanding of unconscious dynamics in behavior and appreciation for experiential learning, as well as a high regard for the uniqueness of each patient. He also points out that modern hypnotherapy is quite different from the popular concept of hypnosis as a mysterious drama. Therapists who employ clinical hypnosis in their practices are not stage artists. Erickson (1977) maintains that in hypnotherapy it is necessary to protect patients and approach them slowly in an effort to help them understand certain events taking place. He also advocates treatment at an unconscious level, but feels patients should be given an opportunity to transfer their insights to the conscious mind as needed.

HYPNOTHERAPY FOR PSYCHOTHERAPISTS

There is no doubt that many hypnotherapists have treated other psychotherapists. With the exception of random cases by Erickson, as described by Haley (1967), there is a paucity of literature on the subject. It is my perception that therapists have been treated quite often with hypnosis and their cases even cited in books and journals, but their professional identities were not revealed. Perhaps this is because the medical and mental health communities still look askance at this particular treatment approach.

Within the medical center milieu, psychiatry residents, psychology interns, staff psychiatrists and psychologists, and professional social workers can be exposed to the utilization of hypnosis with individuals, families, and groups. Groups, in particular, are quite popular with therapists. I conduct two such groups. The first is an Autohypnosis Group aimed at eliminating such habit problems as smoking, overeating, and insomnia. The second is entitled "The Balanced Life Group" and focuses more on physical and psychophysiological problems for pain management and control. Both groups combine clinical hypnosis with behavior modification. Fezler and Kroger (1976) discuss such an approach with their hypnobehavioral model in the treatment of phobias as well as obsessive compulsive, depressive, and hypochondriacal disorders. In the groups, problems are addressed from an unconscious perspective via heterohypnosis (hypnosis with others) and autohypnosis (self-hypnosis) as well as from a conscious viewpoint by way of modifying behavior through regular exercise, play, diet, and setting immediate and long-term goals.

Quite often staff members and psychotherapy residents or interns from the different disciplines will ask to be seen individually or in the groups as a means of "learning hypnosis to apply to our clinical practice." After all, "such a tool will be invaluable to our repertoire of treatment modalities." At times these therapists are genuinely seeking to learn an additional approach to help them with their patients. At other times they are verbalizing their desire for self-growth. With few exceptions, they are also asking for therapy under the guise of learning a particular skill. By virtue of its composition, the environment of a medical center is oriented towards the incessant quest for and acquisition of knowledge. Seeking the hypnotherapist either individually for "an hour's lesson" or in one of the groups as a "participant-observer" affords a safe channel through which professionals can learn about themselves.

Such an attitude is reinforced by the hypnotherapist who will often relate that in order to learn hypnotic skills effectively, clinicians must first select a problem area, physical or emotional, and begin work on it. In this treatment context the therapists are given the permission they need to concentrate on themselves within their own environment, with few questions asked by their professional colleagues. For example, a resident can say openly that he or she has decided to go through the balanced life or autohypnosis group or "visit" with this therapist one hour a week in order to learn hypnosis. Coping with headaches, anxiety, weight loss, surgical procedures, arousal level to enhance job performance, phobias, and close interpersonal relationships are just a few of the myriad physical, psychological, and psychophysiological complaints that often motivate therapists to seek treatment. These clinicians soon become comfortable with the rationale that it is permissible, even desirable, to acknowledge their personal problems in order to better learn hypnosis as an adjunct to psychotherapy—and all for the sake of education! Such a defense, in the service of the ego, is often unconscious; I think it is a necessary mechanism by which clinicians can ask for help from another therapist and still maintain their professional dignity.

Case 1

One experienced therapist approached me regarding the use of hypnosis for nausea while piloting a plane. He had recently invested in flying lessons and experienced nausea only when piloting the plane over long distances. After several hypnosis sessions it became evident that the nausea was more associated with his troubled marriage than his cross-country trips in an airplane. Flying over many miles of open land was symbolic of his need to be free of his perceived marital prison.

Case 2

Several years ago a staff member asked me about the possibility of autohypnosis for purposes of relaxation. At the time he was being considered for a discharge from the military owing to a possible diagnosis of organic brain syndrome. There was a great deal of discrepancy between his neurological tests, which proved negative, and his neuropsychological tests, which indicated serious organic deficits. The officer proved to be a good hypnotic subject, and went beyond relaxation to control his arousal during reexamination. While in hypnosis he was able to achieve a marked difference in his performance, which also changed the diagnosis from an organic brain syndrome to an atypical learning disability/developmental disorder. He was subsequently retained in the Air Force. A portion of his testing is shown in Figure 1. The first

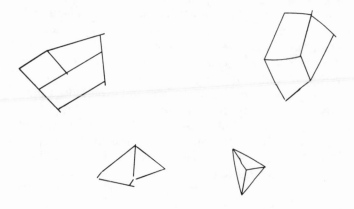

**Attempted drawing of
a cube and pyramid
prior to hypnosis**

**Drawing of a cube
and pyramid while in
hypnosis**

FIGURE 1. Arousal control to enhance performance in a learning disability/developmental disorder. Drawings and spatial arrangements are reproductions of those made by the patient.

drawing represents his repeated but futile efforts to draw a cube and a pyramid. These attempts were made prior to his being in hypnosis and controlling his arousal. He spent ten frustrated and unsuccessful minutes trying to draw the geometric figures. The second drawing was made while in a somnambulistic (deep) and amnesic (without memory or recall of action) state of hypnosis. With the arousal under control, there was marked improvement in his performance; with no hesitation or difficulty he was able to draw the cube and pyramid quickly (several seconds).

Case 3

A reputable female therapist I had known for several years and to whom I had referred cases in the civilian community approached me about her difficulty in forming close, intimate relationships with men. She felt hypnosis might help her become more comfortable in her relationships. She also expressed that trust was a sensitive issue for her and indicated that she had a great deal of confidence in me because of what she had heard from our mutual clientele. She was quite responsive to hypnoanalysis, and within a brief, seven-session period she discovered that she had strong repressed feelings that perhaps she had experienced incestuous relations with her father at an early stage in the latency period. Being bright and motivated, as well as quite suggestible, she experienced revivication (reliving) of a scene from her past in which she and her father were lying in bed together. As she magnified the picture by way of a zoom lens on a camera she saw and experienced that her father was only cuddling her; and ideomotor responses (unconscious finger signals) revealed she had been harboring a distorted fantasy and not reality at all. She obtained immediate intrapsychic relief, which led to a closer relationship with her father and subsequent meaningful relationships with male suitors.

Case 4

I was recently approached by a well-respected psychotherapist who had a sincere desire to lose weight. She, too, was well aware of my hypnotherapy work within the medical center. As is often the case, her innermost feelings were accelerated while she was in hypnosis. In an emotional and enriching session, this bright and intuitive clinician allowed herself to discover what her unconscious was already wrestling with. She had to confront the reality that her weight was intricately mingled with her need for nurturance from her immediate family. Because of the nature of our relationship, she agreed to pursue this further with another hypnotherapist.

RELUCTANCE, RESISTANCE, AND TECHNIQUE

It has been my experience that most mental health professionals, who are not familiar with hypnotherapy, tend to perceive this clinical tool with much the same illusions as the lay person. This is particularly true of the utilization of the unconscious mind while one is in a hypnotic state. Many therapists who do practice hypnotherapy will often refrain from utilizing the unconscious. Sometimes this is owing to a lack of training; at other times it is because their particular treatment philosophy is opposed to it. At still other times it is because of the lack of concrete scientific data to support this phenomenon. It is my opinion that such practitioners can make little progress without acknowledging the intrinsic value of the unconscious. Inability to deal directly and to learn to negotiate with this part of our mind is tantamount to the pursuit of any treatment approach/modality without first acquiring certain basic skills in that area. In the mental health profession clinicians become quite familiar with unconscious conflicts and resistances. For most, this phenomenon is a hidden, intangible force to be reckoned with only in a distant, complicated, and often frustrating endeavor. The competent hypnotherapist employs graphic and direct means of communicating with the unconscious that often facilitate resolution of problems. I feel that such a skill also differentiates hypnotherapy from other forms of suggestive therapy.

There are many ways of uncovering or communicating with the unconscious, and these are readily available in most books and journals on clinical hypnosis. Among the most common are ideomotor finger signals, automatic writing, automatic drawing, automatic typing, and verbal responses. In isolated cases I have observed patients communicate unconscious responses through various colors. LeCron (1971) explains and clarifies seven specific psychodynamic areas in problematic behavior. He labels these conflict, motivation or secondary gain, prior suggestion, organ or body language, identification, masochism or self-punishment, and past experience. He then combines the knowledge of these seven areas with the techniques of uncovering mentioned in order to locate and deal with emotional difficulties effectively. To facilitate this, Cheek and LeCron (1968) advocate involuntary ideomotor finger signals from patients to indicate "Yes; No; I do not know; and I will not say" while they are in hypnosis. These therapists contend, and I agree, that the unconscious mind in hypnosis can meaningfully answer questions that it is unable to while in the conscious or waking state.

Case 5

Several months before transferring from Wilford Hall to another hospital, a nurse practitioner came to me seeking help for an increasing fear of thunderstorms. She related that she had always had some discomfort during storms but that recently her feelings had become more irrational and were quickly approaching phobic dimensions. Such feelings were most definitely creating obstacles to her job and life-style. She was also experiencing extreme difficulty driving to and from the hospital during the storms. On occasion, she would resort to having someone else drive her or waiting out the turbulence. It was also impossible for her to get out socially or perform routine tasks during this type of weather. She felt it ironic that her fears had increased since her new marriage of three months, because she thought being married would reduce her anxiety. When questioned consciously about experiences she associated with her fear, she related one experience at the age of fifteen in which lightning had flashed through her home and superficially grazed her arm. Other than this event, there was no other recollection of a problem. The patient proved to be an excellent hypnotic subject, and under hypnosis exhibited strong ideomotor finger signals. When asked if her unconscious was aware of a past experience related to storms her "yes" finger responded. When asked if this was the same experience she had described at age fifteen, the "no" finger reacted. When asked if this experience had occurred before the age of fifteen there was another "yes" signal. Other "yes" responses were given when asked the same question about ages of before ten and six. The patient then spontaneously age-regressed to age five and she described extreme discomfort in the presence of her parents, who were having a serious quarrel. Asked if she wanted to tell me about it she replied verbally "no" and her involuntary ideomotor signal was the same. I asked if she would prefer we leave the subject alone for awhile, and she responded positively. Later, outside of hypnosis, the patient recalled her parents having an argument, but could not consciously tell me specifics about the incident. In a rather insouciant manner she then stated she felt they had experienced a "stormy marriage" at that time of her life, but fortunately had resolved their difficulties. I then asked if she had ever used the word "stormy" to describe her parents' earlier years of marriage, and she replied that she had not. Further ideomotor questioning led to the fact that she feared her new marriage might also become "stormy." The thunderstorms, of course, represented a diversion from this unwanted thought. Reassurance from her new spouse and the insight she gained from hypnosis brought a quick cessation of her fear. Several months later she was still doing well and reported she had intentionally gone shopping and had socialized during several thunderstorms.

It should be clarified that many patients seek therapy but do not require intense uncovering techniques because they do not have serious and repressed unconscious conflicts. Although ideomotor signaling may initially be helpful to rule out any serious difficulties in these cases, relearning or reprogramming by way of positive imagery and behavior modification is all that is needed.

Case 6

One psychiatric resident discovered the value of combining ideomotor responses with imagery. This physician had originally requested to meet with me one hour a week to learn hypnosis for purposes of self-relaxation and therapy with his patients. Within several sessions it had become apparent that during his on-call days his arousal would escalate and thereby reduce his performance. While in hypnosis he was asked to visualize a scale from one to ten with one being very calm and ten quite excited. By way of ideomotor finger responses he discovered he was functioning at the seven level while imaging himself during on-call days. He was amazed to find that through ideomotor signals he could raise and lower his arousal by raising and lowering the numbers on the scale. On his on-call days his unconscious revealed his arousal often remained at the seven level and would even escalate to an eight level when he left the hospital for home. This obviously began to affect his family life as well. Through hypnotic cognitive rehearsal (imagery conditioning) techniques and posthypnotic suggestions, the resident soon learned to lower his arousal, which subsequently had a positive impact on his job and home life. It should be noted that his hypnosis sessions were combined with having him simultaneously manage his stress in a more well-rounded manner.

Case 7

Another psychiatric resident, who was on heavy dosages of medication for vascular headaches, learned to decrease both the intensity and frequency of his malady through hypnotherapy. This resident was also surprised to find himself communicating with his unconscious through involuntary finger responses. While in hypnosis his forefinger responded "yes" to whether or not his headaches were directly correlated to stress. On a scale between one and ten with one signifying "no pain" and ten indicating "great pain," his responses were initially at the eight level. Later, as he learned to modify his behavior and work on his stress, his involuntary finger movements indicated a considerable reduction on the scale. Although his headaches have been allayed, he continues to use his ideomotor responses as a gauge to his stress and pain.

Psychotherapists, particularly analysts, are reluctant to use hypnotherapy because of the antiquated notion that it accomplishes only temporary symptom removal. They cling to the rationale that the underlying factors causing such symptoms are untouched and that the original symptoms will either return or be replaced by even worse ones. Freud, of course, perpetuated much of this belief with his simple approach of suggesting symptoms away and his subsequent failures to be able to do so. In the past, lack of time, training, and exposure in medical and graduate schools were other reasons why practitioners were reluctant to utilize hypnotherapy. Fortunately the two national societies mentioned earlier, ASCH and SCEH, and their respective journals are currently instrumental in educating professionals and providing valuable literature in the field of hypnotherapy.

In the treatment of therapists I have encountered resistance around the issue of conscious control. With few exceptions, psychotherapists tend to possess all the qualities of good hypnotic subjects. They are usually bright, motivated, and creative individuals who apply these characteristics in their personal and professional lives. These same strengths of character can also work for them in hypnotherapy, but they are often used, particularly in the early phases of treatment, to thwart the efforts of the hypnotherapist. In their enthusiasm these professional patients will frequently question both themselves and their therapist regarding every minute detail they encounter. Such inquiry tends to force conscious screening or interference in the beginning sessions. Of course, the therapists are generally unaware that they are impeding therapy by their inquisitiveness.

I welcome early and overt resistance and perceive it as a healthy signal in most patients.

Case 8

One therapist was eager to learn hypnosis for purposes of alleviating tension in himself as well as using the tool with his patients. He was an extremely compulsive individual, and after several minutes of the first induction he opened his eyes and blurted out "I do not feel any different than I did when we first began." After several sessions he continued to demonstrate his doubts in a rather obstreperous fashion. I then questioned if he was really interested in learning hypnosis for himself and his practice. He assured me he was genuinely motivated but could not seem to relax with the method. The point was emphasized that one does not always have to relax in hypnosis, as is true in other types of therapy. The patient was also made aware that there were no expectations of him and that, in fact, he had achieved altered states many times in his life throughout his childhood, in his academic pursuits, and even in his practice. He was then instructed to close his eyes and "not try to do anything." He could "either listen to me or not listen to me; it does not make any difference." Also, any external thoughts were just further signals for him to enjoy himself. I then proceeded to give a long and monotonous discourse on how persons learn to be unconscious in their activities from childhood through adult life. The patient soon achieved a good, medium trance state.

After the hypnotic experience he related that he had become quite bored with my voice and drifted into a dream state similar to that he experienced while asleep. In his altered state he recalled a persistent dream in which he was a news anchorman on a nightly television show. Since he could easily capture this scene, I asked him to close his eyes again and do so. Within seconds he again found himself in a sound hypnotic state. He later expressed surprise that he could achieve hypnosis so quickly and that it was so similar to a dream state he had been experiencing for years.

This early apprehension can often be harnessed and channeled constructively by the skilled hypnotherapist as he or she meets the resistance with skills of diverting the conscious and utilizing more indirect suggestions. Kroger (1963) sees the diversion of conscious attention as the key to a successful hypnotic state and uses it extensively in both clinical and forensic areas of his practice. Erickson (1960) was a master at misdirecting conscious energy and giving indirect suggestions. Coué (1923), an early pioneer in the field, was another strong proponent of the nonspecific suggestion, since he felt most patients would receive it uncritically. He also found it helpful to attach a strong emotion to the suggestion. In addition, Coué's suggestions would emphasize only the goal rather than a means of getting there.

There are also clinicians who utilize more direct suggestions. Crasilneck (1975) makes excellent use of commands in his work, giving direct and sometimes quite negative suggestions to his patients. The Spiegels (1978) offer numerous examples of direct suggestions and without application of the uncovering process. I prefer the features of misdirection of conscious attention, indirect suggestion, attaching a strong emotion to the suggestion, and emphasis on the results of a goal in dealing with professionals and their conscious resistance. Once therapists sense they are not giving up control but are actually gaining more control, their critical conscious screening begins to diffuse. When this occurs they are then in a position to take further advantage of their inner strengths.

Case 9

A staff physician asked if I would see her prior to major surgery. She wanted to learn autohypnosis for purposes of deep relaxation and easing presurgical anxiety. Although she had taken a few courses on the subject, she was still quite skeptical about its merits. However, at the time she was "willing to try anything." Since she had grown up on an island in the Pacific Ocean, it was quite easy for her to imagine a beach scene for purposes of the induction. When questioned about a particular sensation or feeling, she immediately replied she felt warm and secure. I then began a monologue on how nice it was to take time out from the busy roller coaster of life and drift peacefully, placidly, comfortably along. It was then suggested that her warmth and security had always been with her and would continue to be with her no matter where she went or what she did. Outside hypnosis the patient reported immediate relaxation. After only two sessions she was able to develop anesthesia in various parts of her body. Her new ability not only prepared her for surgery, but helped her during and afterwards.

This case also made use of imagery by having the subject fixate her conscious mind on a pleasurable interest while suggestions were given to her at the unconscious level. Although the skilled clinician can utilize imagery without hypnosis and hypnosis without imagery, it is my opinion that the combination of the two is most productive in countering conscious resistance, particularly in the early phases of treatment. The use of imagery is widespread not only in hypnotherapy but also in behavior therapy. Approximately twenty-five years ago, Wolpe (1958) described how persons could reduce their phobic condition merely by way of imagery and indicated that they did not have to be actively in the presence of the phobic stimulus. Erickson's interspersal technique (1966) often has the patient vacillate between neutral imagery (pleasant scenes) and suggested imagery (pain management, emotional well-being) to reduce conscious critical screening. Fezler and Kroger (1976) show how their patients, in the hypnotized state, utilize positive fantasies to see themselves correcting their problems. Abramovitz and Lazarus (1962) demonstrate how positive imagery serves to countervail phobic reactions. In fact, Lazarus (1977) has presented a myriad of innovative and creative uses of imagery in therapeutic situations. Simonton (Creighton, Simonton, & Simonton 1978), in his provocative work with cancer patients, has them move from a pleasant scene to one in which they image their immune system combating the illness. Many professionals use the terms covert rehearsal or covert conditioning to describe imagery. For example, Cautela (1975) uses these words to describe how he combines imagery with behavior modification to treat phobias, alcoholism, and sexual disorders. In treating psychotherapists, I prefer the interspersing or vacillating technique of cognitive imagery combined with active modification of behavior as the most cogent means of dealing with the often-unruly conscious will.

In an effort to facilitate the hypnotic process, I spend a great deal of time with therapists exploring their particular individual cue words or sensations. The therapist's inattention to such valuable gateways can lead to patient frustration. It has been my experience that all patients experience uniquely different cues to help them relax and/or go deeper into hypnosis. I prefer to use their own personal and instinctive hints rather than some general clues they may have read or heard. For some individuals these guides may involve different colors or the same color; for others, certain words may be a key; and for still others, certain sounds and/or feelings may create a sense of well-being. Sometimes it is a combination of several of these. Ideally, these comfortable signals are located early in therapy, but many persons have to struggle to find them. While patients are in hypnosis, I often make the suggestion that their unconscious minds will spontaneously find the cue that is most secure for them. To the surprise of patients this is a rather frequent occurrence: "While my eyes were closed this purple triangle just popped into my head"; "I felt a sudden glow or warmth"; "This relaxed heaviness or lightness just covered me like a blanket." When this phenomenon does occur I will have them immediately return to the hypnotic state by using their personal key. Again conscious energy is being distracted and the unconscious becomes receptive to further stimuli. My opinion is that such cues are extremely valuable and necessary assets to both the misdirection of conscious attention and to interspersal imagery in dealing with control issues of mental health professionals.

SUMMARY

Hypnotherapy, particularly in a major medical center, can offer psychotherapists a rich and rewarding experience under the heading of treatment and/or training. Through the guidance of the skilled hypnoclinician, staff, residents, and interns in the various disciplines can take advantage of a creative and unique form of therapy with little or no stigmatizing by their peers. With judicious acceptance of the unconscious phenomena that often occur during hypnotherapy, practitioners can take enormous strides in facilitating their own treatment or in working with their patients. If they concurrently take advantage of the national and international exposure to hypnotherapy they place themselves in an even stronger position to enhance their learning. With frequent practice of the various hypnotic techniques mentioned, psychotherapists can become more proficient with hypnotherapy in their personal lives and in the lives of those they treat.

References

Abramovitz, A. & Lazarus, A. The use of "emotive imagery" in the treatment of children's phobias. *Journal of Mental Science,* 1962, *108*:109.

Bramwell, J. M. *Hypnotism: Its history, practice and therapy.* New York: Julian Press, 1956.

Bromberg, W. *Man above humanity.* Philadelphia: J. B. Lippincott, 1954.

Cautela, J. R. The use of covert conditioning in hypnotherapy. *International Journal of Clinical & Experimental Hypnosis,* 1975, *23*, 15–27.

Cheek, D. B., & LeCron, L. M. *Clinical hypnotherapy.* New York: Grune & Stratton, 1968.

Conn, J. On the history of hypnosis. In *Introductory Lectures on Medical Hypnosis.* The Institute of Research in Hypnosis, 1958, 80–89.

Coué, E. *How to practice suggestion and autosuggestion.* New York: American Library Service, 1923.

Crasilneck, H. B. & Hall, J. A. *Clinical hypnosis principles and applications.* New York: Grune & Stratton, 1975.

Creighton, J., Simonton, O. C., & Simonton, S. M. *Getting well again.* Los Angeles: J. P. Tarcher, 1978.

Cutten, G. B. *Three thousand years of mental healing.* New York: Scribner, 1911.

Edelstein, G. M. *Trauma, trance and transformation: A clinical guide to hypnotherapy.* New York: Brunner/Mazel, 1981.

Erickson, M. H. Special techniques of brief hypnotherapy. *Journal of Clinical & Experimental Hypnosis,* 1960, *8*, 3–16.

Erickson, M. H. The interpersonal hypnotic technique for symptom correction and pain control. *American Journal of Clinical Hypnosis,* 1966, *8*, 198–209.

Erickson, M. H. Hypnotic approaches to therapy. *American Journal of Clinical Hypnosis,* 1977, *20*, 20–35.

Erickson, M. H., Rossi, E. L., & Rossi, S. I. *Hypnotic realities.* New York: Irvington Publishers, 1976.

Fezler, W., & Kroger, W. S. *Hypnosis and behavior modification.* Philadelphia: J. B. Lippincott, 1976.

Greenberg, Ira A. (Ed.). *Group hypnotherapy and hypnodrama.* Chicago, Ill.: Nelson-Hall, 1977.

Haley, J. (Ed.). *Advanced techniques of hypnosis and therapy: Selected papers of Milton H. Erickson, M. D.* New York: Grune & Stratton, 1967.

Kline, M. V. *Clinical correlations of experimental hypnosis.* Springfield, Ill.: Charles C. Thomas, 1963.

Kroger, W. S. *Clinical and experimental hypnosis in medicine, dentistry, and psychology.* Philadelphia: J. B. Lippincott, 1963 & 1967.

Lazarus, A. *In the mind's eye.* New York: Rawson Associates, 1977.

LeCron, L. M. *The complete guide to hypnosis.* New York: Barnes and Noble Books, 1971.

Rosen, G. History of medical hypnosis. In J. M. Schneck (Ed.), *Hypnosis in Modern Medicine*. Springfield, Ill.: Charles C. Thomas, 1959.

Spiegel, D., and Spiegel, H. *Trance and management: Clinical uses of hypnosis*. New York: Basic Books, 1978.

Wolberg, L. *Medical hypnosis*. New York: Grune & Stratton, 1951.

Wolpe, J. *Psychotherapy in reciprocal inhibition*. California: Stanford University Press, 1958.

EDITOR'S COMMENTARY

Another Route toward Knowing Thyself

Because Churchill is probably one of the few people in this country based in an interdisciplinary training setting who both directs a unit for hypnotherapy and practices it, and whose clientele is composed largely of therapy trainees and practitioners, he brought a vast amount of knowledge, experience, and insight to writing this chapter. The many referrals he receives from his medical colleagues plus the self-referrals of staff and interns attest to the respect for his competence. During my several week-long stays at Wilford Hall as a Distinguished Visiting Professor in the past few years, it became quite obvious to me that Churchill is considered an outstanding "therapist's therapist."

He elucidates a phenomenon alluded to in several other chapters—namely, that many clinicians, both neophyte and experienced, frame their request for hypnotherapy in the form of seeking knowledge of the technique as part of their education. And indeed it is and becomes an aspect of their experiential training! But what is also significant is the denial, conscious or unconscious, of the desire for therapy qua therapy to deal with some personal problems or issues—perhaps more rapidly and in what they assume is a more disguised way. Why does this denial that therapy is being sought for therapeutic reasons surface so often? Is it because despite the field's spoken avowal of its importance as a core training component in many, but definitely not all programs, there is still a stigma attached to really "needing" therapy? Perhaps we are still so involved in old concepts of illness, pathology and dysfunction, and long-term treatment that the growth-producing, greater health potential inherent in some therapies, including brief therapy, is overlooked. More emphasis on the latter might enable therapists to enter treatment more realistically for personal and professional gain.

Churchill persuasively makes the case for hypnotherapy as an intervention strategy in its own right as well as an adjunct to other therapies. Its particular value of being able to break through rapidly to central disturbing material commends its usage for those who want and can tolerate its rapid, surgery-like, precise entry. Fortunately, as Churchill indicates, clients will not delve into material with which they are not yet ready to deal, nor will they behave in therapy in ways that are truly ego dystonic. The wonder of personality is this built-in safety defense system.

Wisely, Churchill cautions that practitioners of this healing art, as of all other forms, should be extremely well trained and professionally allied with one of the two major national hypnotherapy professional organizations. For, ultimately, the currency in which we are all dealing is human lives, and this is, indeed, precious stuff.

5

Treatment of Marital and Family Therapists

Florence W. Kaslow, PH.D.

Some years ago the phone rang one afternoon and the following conversation ensued:

P.G.: Hi! Any chance you have some free time tonight?
F.K.: Yes, when would you like to come over? It's a free evening.
P.G.: About 8:00 P.M. It will probably take several hours, so I'm glad we won't be hurried.

Since Phil* was a professional colleague with whom I was to present a paper at a conference, I assumed he was coming over to begin writing. For several weeks we had been trying to arrange a convenient time, and this had fallen into place well. Thus, when he arrived and indicated that he was having severe marital difficulties, and his intent in the phone call was to be making an appointment for a marathon therapy session, I was astounded. He indicated that since he knew every therapist in our geographic area (which was quite true), he had either to travel very far or to select someone he knew. He had decided to turn to me since he had high regard for my therapeutic skill based on his having referred patients to me and having received good feedback, having observed my work directly when I did teaching-demonstrations at workshops and on videotapes, having discussed our philosophies of therapy and patient care and finding a high level of agreement,

---

*Initials and names have been changed to protect the identity of the therapist/patient and his wife.

and knowing that I held to very stringent rules regarding confidences of friends and colleagues as well as patients. In addition, he felt his wife respected me and would be more apt to join him in therapy with me than any of their other therapist acquaintances. Further, he thought that because I knew them, I could zero in more rapidly on the dilemma and help them reach some resolution in the near future so they could avoid "therapy interminable."

I pointed out the difficulties likely to be inherent in therapy with him, and if she agreed to join him, with them. These included that his wife might expect that I would be partial to him, as the major connective link was through our professional ties; that our collegial interaction would have to diminish during the course of therapy, so that the primary current relationship would revolve around the therapy (and I had some reluctance to set aside our proposed writing and speaking collaboration); and that since I already knew them, my impressions would not be as fresh and uncontaminated as if they were stranger-patients.

Since he was a senior clinician, he was well aware of these problems. But given that he had long been professionally active in the community, he would have run into similar difficulties with any other senior therapist in the area, and he did not wish to go to a new, junior person. Thus, we agreed to try a few sessions and then reconsider if a therapeutic alliance was indeed feasible.

During that evening's two-hour session, our relationship subtly shifted as he poured out his frustration and turmoil and as I responded as a clinician instead of as a friend to "his story." The next day his wife called, at his request. Since my philosophy of marital therapy recognizes the importance of balance, I offered her a comparable two-hour session alone. She accepted; "her story" (Duhl, 1981) unfolded about her dismay over their bitter conflicts, her recognition that he was so dissatisfied and had already moved away from her emotionally, and her suspicion that he was involved with someone else. She had long wanted to enter treatment, but he had refused, not wishing to make their private life known to anyone in our large yet semi-incestuously intertwined professional world. She was relieved that he had finally sought assistance, and recognized that it would inevitably be with someone they knew; coming to me was acceptable to her as "the vibes had always been good."

After six conjoint marital sessions, the irrefutable fact that became clear was that he felt he had "done time" by staying in the marriage as long as he had and that their differences were both untenable and irreconcilable for him. He had stayed "imprisoned" because he wanted to wait until their two children had finished high school and also because he was ashamed that even though a marital therapist himself, he could not resolve his own problems and did not like exhibiting his failure to the world in the form of separation and divorce. She was devastated, and bitterly confronted him about the rumors circulating that he was having an affair. In sheer desperation, and apparently hoping that his affirmation that he was would disgust her enough that she would more rapidly agree to a divorce, he confessed that indeed he had been involved for quite a while. She caught me off guard when she turned and angrily hurled the following at me:

M.G.: You sit there so smugly! You have such a great understanding! Are you the culprit? And you pretend to be objective! How dare you—"professional friends!" Do you expect me to believe that?

F.K.: I hope you will believe it. I understand your concern and am distressed by it. But I can reassure you my friendship with your husband is professional and not sexual. [This statement was true, which was why I was nonplussed for a few seconds by her suspicion. Also she had originally agreed to enter into therapy with me stating that she trusted me and my skill.]

P.G.: There you go again—lashing out—blaming the wrong person—not accepting responsibility for your coldness and possessiveness as the factors that drove me away! I don't sleep with all of my female friends! Damn it, how can you think I'd ask Florrie to be our therapist if she were my lover? I'm not and never have been a manipulative cad.

By the end of this tense and turbulent session, he indicated he would begin apartment hunting the next day and move out as quickly as possible—preferably within the week. I queried if she felt she could continue working with me around the separation, given her suspicions. She rejoined that she wanted to think about it, which was certainly understandable. She called a few days later. She wanted to return immediately as she felt desperately in need of empathy and support and was abashed about her vindictive attack on me.

I continued working with them individually through the separation and legal divorce, trying to help them through their anger, bitterness, resentment, and sense of failure (Kaslow, 1981). She also had to cope with the desolation of being "unwanted," rejected by a man she still loved and saw as a very important person. She did not look forward to being single; she had liked her married lifestyle. He wanted "out" quickly, was willing to be generous in a settlement to exonerate himself from some of his guilt, and wanted very much to be able to see his girlfriend openly post-divorce, as their clandestine relationship troubled him. M.G.'s depression lasted many months, as did her desire to retaliate for the hurt and humiliation he caused her.

Once the legal divorce was finalized and the economic divorce agreed upon (Bohannan, 1973; Kaslow, 1983), Mrs. G. began to settle down and accept the marital dissolution as a "fait accompli." In the aftermath period, she began to date and rebuild her life, continuing in treatment several months after her ex-husband had felt finished and had terminated.

This first instance of treating another therapist and his partner caused me to ponder the intricacies of this process. It seemed similar to, yet also different from, other therapies I conducted. I was certain that I felt a little more anxious, a little more desirous that the outcome be "successful," whatever that meant, and a little more concerned because covertly I felt I, too, had more at stake in treating a mental health professional who knew a great deal about therapy after years as an artful practitioner and supervisor and who could potentially be hypercritical. I was conscious of being more attuned to boundary issues and ambivalently intrigued about potential competitive strivings if the therapist-patient should try to become cotherapist. Also at risk was a friendship I treasured. Perhaps the initial tap root for this book was planted when that case commenced and periodically during its course when I reconsidered the efficacy of treating them.

Subsequently, while still living in Philadelphia, I found my practice included an increasing number of therapists as patients with their spouses and, often, their nuclear or extended families. Since my relocation to Florida in 1980, this trend has continued so that currently close to one third of my patients are other therapists. In age they range from 28 to 55; about half the therapists are men and half are women; there are roughly equal numbers of psychiatrists, psychologists, and social workers. The question of why and how some individuals become identified as therapists' therapists and others are never sought out by their colleagues continues to fascinate me. The following material—which shifts among ideas presented in the literature, clinical vignettes, and observations and assumptions drawn from colleague input and patient responses—represents an attempt to look at this issue, particularly regarding the modality of marital and family therapy.

MANDATORY THERAPY AS PART OF TRAINING: TO BE OR NOT TO BE

Traditionally, the field of psychoanalysis has required that anyone in training to be an analyst must undergo a full didactic analysis. This is to combine therapeutic aspects as well as learning components. One's own analysis was and is today the quintessential way to experience and come to know what analysis consists of, what is involved in exploring the unconscious regions of one's heart, soul, mind, spirit, and cognitive processes. It is believed that a person can not guide an analysand into this interior domain unless one has already personally thoroughly travelled there, abreacted painful events, continued tasks that had been short-circuited by arrested development, and reached a high level of insight, self-acceptance, and comprehension of unconscious as well as conscious processes and motivations (Langs, 1981).

But didactic analyses, like "purely" therapeutic analyses, are costly and time consuming. They may last three to five years and be held four or five times a week. Anyone entering this process must make a major commitment of energy, time, and finances to it. They generally should be prepared not to relocate during this phase of their life since the entire analysis should be conducted by one person. Those who are considered masters of the art of psychoanalysis are dubbed "training analysts," a title much revered. Only a training analyst is deemed qualified to conduct a didactic analysis, so the choices in any community are necessarily limited. Since he or she is likely to earn a substantial portion of his or her total income this way, "professional courtesy" is not the rule, and may be, of necessity, a rarity. Sometimes it is possible to become an analysand of one of the training analysts at an institute; then the fees may be substantially reduced.

What have been and are the implications of this kind of re-

quirement on other segments of the psychotherapeutic community?

During the past 50 years in the United States, the picture has
varied greatly in different departments of psychiatry, psychology,
and social work. Some have "required" individual therapy and
others have "strongly encouraged" it. Conversely, some have been
reluctant to accept students and interns who are in treatment, pur-
porting concern that needing therapy themselves, they may be too
unstable or too self-immersed to be ready and able to focus on and
treat others. Wherein lies the truth? Or are there several truths?

Three questions come to mind:

1. Is it not advisable to experience therapy from the patient's vantage point as one critical aspect of coming to comprehend what
   it means to unveil one's self-doubts, innermost fears and longings, and well-disguised secrets?
2. Should any person embarking on a career as a therapist be deprived of or discouraged from tasting the personal privilege and
   pressures that accompany the therapeutic journey toward self-
   knowledge, personal growth, and improved functioning?
3. Should at least part of one's own journey encompass the modality or modalities one is planning to practice?

My bias is that the answer to the first and third questions is a clear
yes; to the second, a rather definite no.

THERAPY THAT INCLUDES
ONE'S SIGNIFICANT OTHERS

Since the focus of this chapter is specifically marital and family
therapy, let us briefly review some documentation of what has
transpired in the past. In 1968 Nichols wrote a highly informative
article entitled "Personal Psychotherapy for Marital Therapists."
He describes the philosophy of and approach taken at the Merrill-
Palmer Institute's postdoctoral intern training program regarding
resolution of the training-treatment question. During more than 10
years preceding the writing of Nichol's article, the Institute had
carefully delineated a pattern that separated yet coordinated personal psychotherapy and supervision for the interns. Each intern
was assigned by the head of the training program to a primary su-

pervisor who carried the main responsibility for designing the case load to meet training-learning requirements; in addition, he or she was assigned to other supervisors drawn from the Institute's multidisciplinary staff with expertise in other treatment modalities. Another member of the Institute's psychotherapy training faculty, not engaged in supervising the particular intern, was assigned as the psychotherapist (Nichols, 1968, p. 84). The modal number of therapy sessions was two per week, although the requirement was only for one.

Nichols indicated that the unique feature of the program was that treatment was mandatory, that it was provided within and by the training institute, that therapists were assigned rather than selected by the interns, and that much faculty time and energy was invested in coordinating supervision and treatment to maximize the benefits derived from both experiences. Over time, wives of interns were sometimes accepted into treatment by the husband's therapist. (The implication seems to be that all interns there were male then.) Nichols interpreted what appears to have then been a rather progressive development as concrete recognition of "the belief that the intern's own marriage and family life affect his learning and functioning as a psychotherapist and are an integral part of his professional well-being" (p. 84).

That this needed to be posited then because such a realization was not a generally accepted fact or practice seems suprising a decade and a half later. What is even more astonishing is that such involvement of the spouse, even in programs oriented to training skilled marital and family therapists (and not mere technicians) is still the exception, rather than the rule. Rarely is it obligatory; just as rarely is it stated that what happens to the trainee during his or her rigorous and personally demanding graduate or postgraduate training has an impact on the family. The combination of emotional turmoil and disinhibiting that may occur; the soul-searching and self-questioning; the intensive involvement in reading and classroom studies; the mesmerizing qualities of clinical practice; the deep engagement with fellow-trainees, faculty members, supervisors, and therapists all converge to bring about changes in the trainee's attitudes, behavior, personality, and way of being in the world. Sometimes the working through of disagreements with and attachment to a cotherapist can be quite profound and disquieting because of the importance this relationship assumes (Kaslow, 1980). Clearly then, not only does the therapist's family life affect

his training and practice, but his professional development has interpersonal ramifications for his family life.

To return to the illumination of issues provided by Nichols
(1968, p. 85) in discussing the Merrill-Palmer model: confidentiality
was respected assidously. Faculty member/therapists kept the content of treatment sessions private. Nothing could be shared with
other members of the faculty training team without the intern's
permission. Nonetheless, broad understanding of the intern's
strengths and stresses might be "shared with others on the training team at appropriate times," as when a supervisor might ask the
therapist's opinion about pressuring an intern for increased productivity. Also, on occasion, a supervisor might suggest that an issue raised in supervision could be dealt with more appropriately
and beneficially in therapy. Obviously, when therapy is conducted
by a member of a training faculty, great caution must be exercised
to see that boundaries are respected and protected so that trainees
feel safe in the confines of the therapeutic sanctuary.

Nichols (1968, p. 85) made a strong case for the value of including personal therapy as part of the training phase. He posited
that as an integral aspect of the program, it enabled the intern to
make more effective and productive use of the experience. It provided an avenue through which to process the tensions and strains
created in a postgraduate program, such as getting entangled in
struggles with those in authority, trying to manipulate one's supervisors, or coming up against one's own blocks and clinical inef-
fectiveness with patients. Thus, through the therapeutic process,
energy did not remain bound up in these struggles but became
available for learning and clinical tasks. The major intention of the
treatment component for trainees was to enable them to become
more effective professionally, to enhance their ability to intervene
beyond the level of obvious and tangible problems, and to enable
them to be able to risk establishing intense therapeutic alliances,
when appropriate. Their actual personal therapy provided an in
vivo prototypical experience of what therapy is and can be. Restructuring personality and curing psychopathology were not the
key objectives.

In the psychotherapeutic portion of their training, those interns who evidenced severe difficulties in working with patients in
dyads and in being in triangular relationships were helped to ap-
praise their strengths and limitations realistically and perhaps
counseled to remain individual psychotherapists or to "emphasize

the teaching-academic side of [their] vocational identity in the future" (Nichols, p. 87). One can question this latter point based on the idea that one should not teach clinical theory and technique in an arena in which one is not a successful practitioner, able to model one's work and supervise that of trainees from the vantage point of an active, competent clinician.

Given that many training program directors agonize over what to do with bright trainees who do not seem to have the personality potential for becoming clinically adept, dealing with this in therapy appears to be an excellent idea. In therapy, the trainee can be confronted with his or her lack of "goodness of fit," can come to terms with it, and can assume responsibility for career redirection. Some major traumatic hassles could be averted in current training programs. In the decade and a half since Nichols' article was written, counseling out and dropping graduate students and postgraduate trainees for personality factors or lack of clinical aptitude rather than for academic reasons has become extremely problematic; threats of lawsuits for so doing are not uncommon. There are few widely agreed upon objective measures for predicting who will or will not be an effective clinician. Nonetheless, there might be subjective unanimity of faculty that a given trainee is not a good candidate for the field. If this were handled adroitly in both supervision and therapy, how much better able the person might be to integrate this information and use it positively, avoiding seeking recourse for reinstatement through litigation. If the modality is marital therapy for the trainee and spouse, the spouse, too, can express apprehension, confusion, or relief about a recommended change in career direction and feel less like a passive victim.

The issue of marital and family therapy as an obligatory part of the individual's training remains controversial. On the opposite end of the continuum from Nichols, some, like Jay Haley, have asserted that a requirement for personal therapy has no place in the training of family therapists and, in fact, may even be in violation of the trainees' personal rights.[1] The violation of rights is an important ethical consideration that merits attention. It is posited here that if the catalogue for the program indicates that individual and/or marital and family therapy make up an integral and mandatory part of the program, then the applicant can choose whether or not this is a requirement he or she is willing to fulfill. After students have chosen such a program, there is no danger of their

rights being violated. However, if they are not told of this requirement prior to admission, then a complaint of violation of personal
rights could well be justified.

A review of the literature that touches on this topic in a global
way reveals that many trainers and clinicians believe trainees
should enter therapy in order to explore their personal biases,
blocks, and points of arrested development and to achieve greater
insight and growth. Yet, ideas as to the auspices and structure
through which this is to occur are nebulous; thus, the trainee is often in a quandary as to the expectation.

Guldner explicitly spoke to the issue; his stance is quite similar
to Nichols'. In his succinct article, *Family Therapy for the Trainee in
Family Therapy* (1978), Guldner describes the resolution of this
question in the marital and family therapy training program of the
Interfaith Counseling Centre, Kitchener, Ontario, Canada. This
two-year interdisciplinary postdegree training program, begun in
1972, entailed 25 hours per week including course work and eight
hours of patient treatment. Most of the trainees had been in practice for a number of years and had returned specifically to acquire
skill in marital and family therapy. Much individual and group supervision, utilizing direct and indirect methods, is an integral part
of the learning experience.

Initially the teaching and supervisory staff all had a strong
positive bias toward the importance of therapy as part of training,
but they did not make it essential. Soon they became aware of an
interesting phenomenon; those trainees involved in personal in-
depth therapy were increasingly seeing fewer clients conjointly
(Guldner, 1978, p. 128). When asked about this in supervision,
they revealed that they thought there were numerous personal issues to be resolved by clients before they could be involved in marital or family therapy. Rarely was such resistance to conjoint therapy evidenced by trainees who were not in individual therapy. As
a corollary, trainees in individual training also were less receptive
to learning and absorbing the program's general systems theoretical model. Significantly, those trainees whose spouses entered
treatment during the same period saw a different therapist, and no
overtures were made for conjoint sessions. Since few therapists
(besides those on the faculty) practicing in the geographic locale of
the Counseling Centre were trained in a systems orientation, trainees were being treated primarily by therapists adhering to a psychoanalytic model.

Next, they decided to utilize group therapy at the Centre. Although it proved more concordant with the program and successful than individual treatment had been, some nontrainee spouses called for appointments. The consensus was that they felt excluded, jealous, and desirous of a comparable therapeutic or growth experience. At the conclusion of the training phase, some couples called for marital therapy. At that point, the training staff concluded that if the trainees were to have an optimal therapeutic experience consonant with what they were learning and the services they were being prepared to deliver, they should be involved in treatment with their own families.

Out of a successful pilot project, the Centre evolved a flexible model that I think has much to commend it. Applicants were informed, before admission, that there would be a "personal growth/therapy experience as a part of training provided by the Centre staff" and that it would involve significant family members. The specifics were to be worked out in individual contracts between therapist and trainee. Ultimately some entered marital therapy and others entered nuclear family therapy. At times family of origin and intergenerational sessions were held; so, too, were individual sessions. The therapist assigned did not carry supervisory responsibility with the same trainee and had minimal teaching contact. As in the Merrill-Palmer program, confidentiality did not pose a problem, and it appears that potentially confusing and often-feared conflictual overlapping relationships did not surface as a major dilemma.

In addition, in keeping with the Centre's prevention/education thrust in the community, and its inclusion of sex therapy services, all trainees and their spouses were required to be involved in an intensive marriage enrichment experience and in a sexual attitude reassessment experience.

Based on my own experiences during the past 15 years as a clinician and teacher in graduate, postgraduate, and professional training programs, I thoroughly concur with Guldner's conclusion (1978, p. 132):

> The involvement of trainees in marital and family therapy should be an essential component of family therapy training. Training programs in family therapy generally have as learning goals the acquisition of theoretical concepts, techniques, skills and self awareness. Consistent integration of these elements for imple-

mentation in family practice appears, from our data, to come
when the self awareness experiences occur within the context of
the trainees' own marital and family system.

We see it as important that the trainee's own therapy and
training be concurrent and that supervision and therapy are
clearly differentiated by ensuring that the trainee is not supervised by his/her own therapist. We do not think it is essential that
the therapy be provided by the training center staff when this is
not possible, but it is important that the therapeutic and training
models and philosophies do not conflict.

Not every practitioner who wants additional training in marital and family therapy can enter a formal graduate or institute-
based program. Many people who have been in practice for a while
have heavy family and financial responsibilities that they determine preclude half- to full-time enrollment in such programs. Others are unable to relocate to communities that have such programs.
For these reasons, the American Association of Marriage and Family Therapists set up an alternative training route through tutelage
under approved supervisors (AAMFT, 1976).

Case Vignette

Don had his masters in counseling and guidance, and worked as a
school psychologist in a suburban high school. He had become increasingly interested in the family context of the adolescents he
saw, and began reading the relevant family therapy literature. At
age 38, he was the father of four children. The youngest was two
and the eldest 13 when his interest in advanced training became
strong. His wife, Jeanine, did not think she could return to work
for several years, and his salary barely covered the family's essential needs. He worked out a training bloc with an AAMFT supervisor,
and attended many lectures and workshops in the Philadelphia
area, which is rich in outstanding family therapy programs. His supervisor, who urged all trainees to have some marital therapy during the course of training, referred him to me. We contracted for
10 sessions and we hoped that would be enough for him to experience the potential potency of this intervention modality.

Jeanine was reluctant at first, claiming that it was his training
and that she saw no need for her inclusion in this way. For her the
marriage was fine, and she did not want the existing equilibrium
disrupted. Don's underlying restlessness and resentment did

erupt by the third session, as he talked of his desire to go back for his doctorate and his feeling that all of the advanced training, without the title Doctor, would still leave him a second-class citizen in the therapy world with fellow professionals and patients alike. The fourth child had been unplanned, and he haltingly told Jeanine he felt she had trapped him with this last pregnancy because she wanted a large family. Had they stopped with three, she could now work, and he could have enrolled in a graduate program. As he worked through his recriminations, and realized how much he was enjoying the baby and really liked his wife's domesticity, she was able to offer to work part time as a Sunday School teacher and to try to provide some quiet time in which he could read several nights a week. Therapy also focused on issues of self-esteem and competence and how these are intertwined with and separate from titles. He became aware of the mixture of complementary and symmetrical features in their marital relationship. We discussed lifestyle issues and values, and they realized that their basic desires and goals were quite similar; however, there was a disparity in their time tables and how they established priorities. At the end of the 10 weeks, they renegotiated for an additional five sessions since both found that the therapy was enabling them to communicate about heretofore-avoided topics and that they were gaining a deeper understanding and appreciation of each other. Don felt that the merits of conjoint sessions had come alive for him and that the experience of marital therapy had illuminated the process for him. When they ended at the agreed-upon termination date, they had begun renovating the garage for a future private office for Don, who was already licensed as a school counselor, and Jeanine had gotten a Sunday School teaching job at a synagogue. He hoped to apply the following year to a doctoral program that took part-time students. He went on successfully to complete his supervised training for AAMFT clinical membership; his supervisor reported that his clinical work had changed dramatically during the time he was in treatment; he was much more capable of engaging both partners and working with their interactions and transactions.

It appears that trainees learn how to become marital and family therapists not only by reading the literature, observing senior therapists and peers conducting sessions live and on videotape and critiquing them, attending workshops and classes, and seeing couples and families and receiving supervision on their cases, but also by experiencing the treatment process as patients participating with their partners and/or families of origin or procreation. To me it seems that this last factor is every bit as vital in the process as the other four and that its noninclusion constitutes a serious omission.

DIFFICULTIES IN THE MARITAL/FAMILY THERAPIST'S OWN FAMILY SYSTEM

Becoming and being a marital and family therapist is a challenging, exciting, exasperating, provocative, rewarding, and intense experience. From the time one first enters training, through the years of beginning and advanced clinical practice, we analyze why we gravitate toward this field (see for example Ferber, Mendelsohn, & Napier, 1972; Bellak & Faithorn, 1981). We explore and reconnect with our family of origin in any number of ways including doing genograms and making journeys to visit parents and the extended family (Bowen, 1978; Guerin & Fogarty, 1972). We may reevoke and rework our familial bonds through utilization of family photographs, movies, and videotapes (Kaslow & Friedman, 1977).

We learn that this process is never complete. If we pursue it actively, we can bring about a more satisfactory and ethical realignment of our relationship with our parents as we become more adult and can come into fuller possession of our own "personal authority via termination of the intergenerational hierarchical boundary" during the fourth or fifth decade of life (Williamson, 1981). If our parents are deceased, we can acquire "new life at the graveyard" by visiting and completing not only the grief work but also by modifying the nature of the relational ties. Williamson (1978) describes a valuable process to be undertaken at the graveside that can be utilized as a "method of therapy for individuation from a former dead parent." Through all of the reawakening and reexperiencing of our personal historic past, we are often guided to become aware of the "invisible loyalties" to significant biological relatives, particularly our parents, and to be mindful of the ethical-existential obligations that accrue by virtue of their having endowed us with the gift of life (Boszormenyi-Nagy & Spark, 1973) and, it is to be hoped, of love. In many programs trainers, educators, and supervisor trainees pre- and postdegree may encourage or even urge participants to deal with issues related to their family of origin. Pressure from therapeutic impasses encountered with one's own patients also serves as a motivating force to resolve the repressed or smoldering conflicts from childhood and adolescence in self-analysis and in individual or multigenerational therapy.

In the past decade and a half, the literature has given serious consideration to the intergenerational ties, values, battles, cut-offs, renewals, and legacies that shape the personality and practice of the family therapist as clinician. But, until recently, few articles have dealt as specifically with the impact of someone's becoming or being a family therapist on the therapist's family of origin and family of creation. One notable exception is Charny's chapter, "The Personal and Family Mental Health of Family Therapists" (1982). Charny points out that family therapists are no more immune than anyone else to family problems. Rather, there are various influences which impinge on the therapist that are apt to heighten the probability of family dysfunction (1982, p. 14). For example, after listening day after day to others' problems and woes, often seeing progress in small increments, and perhaps sitting in one chair in one room for hours on end, some clinicians are prone to becoming pessimistic and lethargic and to experiencing burnout. Going home after a full day of attentive listening and creative therapeutic interventions, some therapists have exhausted their fund of patience with and empathy for hearing other people's dilemmas (Bellak & Faithorn, 1981). When a male therapist under great stress with extremely difficult patients goes home and his wife wants to talk about even a minor problem, he may irritably grumble or holler that he needs some peace and quiet and complain, "Can't anybody ever respect my wishes?" When the situation to be confonted with the spouse is more serious, havoc can be wreaked when she finds his emotional reservoir depleted. Consider, for example, the S. case.

Case Vignette

Dr. S. was a successful, 31-year-old psychiatrist in the Air Force. He was meticulous, efficient, ambitious, and quite good looking. Seven years before entering therapy with me, he had met a lovely looking young woman, three years his junior. He was then a senior in medical school. She was soft-spoken, reticent, and somewhat dependent. Initially he was attracted to her sweet clinginess, noncompetitiveness, and rather rapid total absorption in his wishes and life dreams. Throughout their two-year, sporadic courtship, he found her shy and demure demeanor appealing and enjoyed her open adoration of him. She felt secure in his strength and decisiveness, needing the anchoring his fastidiousness and structure provided to her low-keyed, drifting style.

After marriage, during the last two years of his residency in psychiatry, she worked in a job as a secretary in a law office. At night he came home excited about the fascination of the intricate world of human behavior as manifested in patient symptomatology and wanted to bubble over about it to her. She came home disgruntled and tired from a pressured day of typing briefs and arranging court calendars. She longed for appreciation, attention, and comfort. He wanted the enthusiastic receptivity he had received in the premarriage phase of their relationship. Neither derived what they sought from the other. Both became increasingly frustrated and annoyed.

Dr. S. began doing family therapy during his last year of residency, and was assigned to do cotherapy with a sensitive yet dynamic female psychology intern. They worked extremely well together, and shared many professional thoughts and interests. Meanwhile, Mrs. S. felt more and more shut out from her husband's new life, and gradually withdrew. Sometimes he came home to blank, aloof silences. Other times there were hysterical, agitated rages to be faced. He was aware of feeling trapped, yet resisted facing the severity of their rift. The more he ignored the difficulties, praying they would disappear, the more distant and frightened Mrs. S. became. They reached a point of living lives of quiet desperation in the same household, with little contact. Dr. S. hoped that once he left his residency and was in the active-duty Air Force, all would change. It did—but for the worse. After he was away on a three-week mission, he came home to find his forlorn wife huddled in a corner. He finally recognized her depression and despair, and took her to a local psychiatrist for treatment that lasted for a year. Meanwhile, they had had no children because of the precarious state of their relationship, but were feeling pressured to start a family by parents and friends and by their own life stage time clock before it became too late.

Finally, one night Mrs. S. had planned a special evening for them, and he called home to cancel saying he would be late because he had a family in crisis. When he came home, he found a cryptic note from his no-longer reticent wife: "Now you have two families in crisis." Alarmed at her acerbic assertiveness, he awaited her return. With great fury she lashed out, telling him he was so busily and selfishly involved in getting trained, becoming proficient, and nurturing his patients and his career that he had reneged on his promises to take care of and cherish her and to nurture their marriage. She chastised that *she* was not the problem, the difficulty was in their relationship, and how come—if he was such an expert in family dynamics—he failed to recognize what had been transpiring in his own domicile? Confronted with such angry accuracy, his blinders fell away, and he agreed to come for marital therapy.

Although this script is derived from an actual case, it closely parallels the scenario of several dozen different therapist couples and families I've seen. It matters not whether the therapist partner is male or female—the issues are similar.

As Charny indicates (1982, p. 42–43), we see that in family therapy, less physical and emotional distance is maintained between the therapist and those participating than in traditional individual therapy. Usually the therapist is sitting in a circle with the family and knows that he or she must in some way "join" the family in order to become an effective change agent. Much of the substance of treatment is interpersonal transactions and deals with universal problems of closeness and distance, individuation and connectedness. Some therapists feel drawn to sharing feelings and material about their own families and engage in considerable self-disclosure. The real-life drama of family living tugs and pulls at one's own humanness and vulnerability; it is not uncommon to see variations on the themes of one's own family being enacted and depicted in one's office. This can lead to genuine encounter of therapist and patients, producing change in all through the painful struggles they share together in the treatment situation. Some therapists have trouble extricating fully from their patient families and carry emotional remnants home with them.

Charny states that from and through family therapy we come to realize that the idea that there can be personal completeness or freedom from problems in intimate relationships is an illusion. Rather, the goal is to cultivate the strength to live out the process of dealing with life's vicissitudes by being true to and comfortable with oneself and being able to work these out in and through the relationship, reconciling differences, accepting imbalances and contradictions, and integrating opposing positions. When one becomes adept at so doing with client families, when one sees the marked positive results, when one is accorded respect and gratitude, it is troublesome to go home to one's own family in which similar conflicts may abound and yet find that the same creative problem-resolution strategies are to no avail and, in fact, are disparaged as "more of your psychology nonsense and jargon."

Given that "the prevailing context in family therapy is clarification of feelings through actual emotional contact," the patients rather quickly experience the gratification and antidote to loneliness of "being with and talking with." As a result, some family therapists carry over to their own families the desire and expectation for the type of ongoing responsiveness and involvement they experience in therapy. Some come to crave and assume dynamic familial interactions and are disappointed by the fear of closeness and lack of continuous dynamic interplay that characterizes their partner and children, who do not spend the day in the intimate atmosphere of the family therapy sanctuary (Charny, 1982, p. 45). Others go home and find the family asking for intensity of involvement, and feel unable to continue functioning with great affectivity after a full day of complex interpersonal relations at work.

Many leaders in the family therapy field have gone through at least one divorce and the wrenching agonies of decisions regarding child custody. For some, the divorce signified failure to make life meaningful in the personal sphere; for others it heralded growth and triumph. Were we able to do some clinical research on their personal family histories and dissatisfactions, we would know much more about the specific kinds of problems family therapists face in their own lives. Given that this data is not available, what follows is based on my own clinical experience and observations and on Charny's material.

ISSUES THAT MAY SURFACE
BEFORE FAMILY THERAPY

The nontherapist spouse may complain of finding the therapist spouse emotionally drained and a poor listener. Or distress may come from the fact that the therapist spouse demands intense interaction and understanding, eschewing phoniness, mediocrity, and boring routines and activities. The nontherapist spouse realizes that his or her mate perceives that by comparison to the family and home, the office, classroom, or workshop is "where the action is" and home can seem like "Dullsville." The therapist spouse often believes he or she has become more sophisticated about child rearing, behavior dynamics, human sexuality, and personality integration, and may disparage the spouse's lack of knowledge on these subjects. Although the therapist spouse wants to deal with relationship issues and make a continuing commitment to growth, the other spouse may be more concerned about reality-oriented concerns like finances, housing, and children's schooling. They emphasize different priorities and may have different focal value systems.

Becoming symptomatic can be a fine way for a nontherapist spouse or the children finally to get attention. This may be what it takes to be interesting and worthy of time and energy. It also provides some clout and leverage to convince the "high and mighty therapist" that his or her own family is in trouble and in need of therapy and/or that therapists are inept and can't even keep their own families functional. Whether rescuer or retaliator, the symptomatic member is likely to precipitate the move into therapy.

THERAPY: A NEW FORM OF FAMILY TOGETHERNESS

Once the family arrives for treatment, the therapist patient is apt to speak first—explaining the family dynamics, structure, and history—allying with the therapist and trying to orchestrate the process. He or she may be embarrassed, defensive, apologetic, overly loquacious, and very uncomfortable. The family is likely to be tense, uncertain in the terrain of the therapist/patient's daily world, and fearing collusion or competition between the treating therapist and the patient/therapist. These issues need to be dealt with early in the therapy so that the focus can remain on the reasons why the family has sought help. The patient/therapist must be assisted in being there as parent, spouse, and family member and not as a cotherapist. Fears regarding confidentiality and loss of professional stature need to be dispelled. If therapist/patient and therapist have other professional interactions, wherever possible these should be suspended or minimized during the course of therapy. For the family, the boundaries should be clarified and demarcated so that no one feels an undue invasion of privacy or fear of exposure.

Once these issues are dealt with and the ideas assimilated, therapy proceeds as it does with other distressed families. Nonetheless, there are some additional considerations. The tendency of the therapist/patient to want to be omniscient and his or her competitive strivings to be "The Doctor" will need to be handled whenever these surface within the context of the family relational pattern and the family-and-therapist system. So, too, wounds to his or her narcissistic pride at being humiliated in front of a therapist colleague by critical family members must be handled. Fear of too much self-disclosure or of not meeting expectations of being a "good" family in therapy are also common manifestations in this patient population.

Allegations likely to be hurled in such families against the therapist/patient by his or her spouse and children are that "you no longer care about us," and "you find others' lives more absorbing and important than ours." Conversely, the therapist spouse may bemoan that patients appreciate his or her concern and counsel and do not take him or her for granted, whereas family disregards his guidance and takes him or her for granted, never saying "thanks" or giving a compliment. High behavioral expectations and perfection and achievement scripts are common in therapists' families. Spouses and children often vaguely feel that they fall short of the ideal vision of the family. Once these tensions are understood, interpreted, and subsequently minimized the therapist and his or her family can embark on the strange and wondrous voyage of family therapy. But it is urgent that the therapist/captain be highly competent, empathic, strong, dynamic, soothing, tactful, confrontative, authentic, and able to win the battle for structure (Napier & Whitaker, 1978) early in the therapeutic journey. Perhaps it is the therapists who gain reputations for possessing the artful combination of all of the above, like Carl Whitaker, who are privileged to become the family therapists for therapists and their families.

References

American Association of Marriage and Family Counselors, *The approved supervisor*. Claremont, Calif.: AAMFC, 1976.

Bellak, L. with Faithorn, P. *Crises and special problems in psychoanalysis and psychotherapy*. New York: Brunner/Mazel, 1981.

Bohannan, P. The six stations of divorce. In M. E. Lasswell and T. E. Lasswell (Eds.), *Love, marriage and family: A developmental approach*. Illinois: Scott, Foresman and Company, 1973.

Boszormenyi-Nagy, I. & Spark, G. *Invisible loyalties*. New York: Harper and Row, 1973.

Bowen, M. *Family therapy in clinical practice*. New York: Jason Aronson, 1978.

Charny, I. W. The personal and family mental health of family therapists. In F. W. Kaslow (Ed.), *The international book of family therapy*. New York: Brunner/Mazel, 1982.

Duhl, F. The use of the chronological chart in general systems family therapy. *Journal of Marital and Family Therapy*, 1981, 7, (3), 345–352.

Ferber, A., Mendelsohn, M., & Napier, A. *The book of family therapy*. New York: Science House, 1972.

Guerin, P. and Fogarty, T. Study your own family. In A. Ferber, M. Mendelsohn, & A. Napier (Eds.), *The Book of Family Therapy*. New York: Science House, 1972.

Guldner, C. A. Family therapy for the trainee in family therapy. *Journal of Marital and Family Therapy*, January 1978, 4, (1), 127–132.

Kaslow, F. W. Some emergent forms of non traditional sexual combinations: A clinical view. *Interaction*. Spring 1980, 3, (1), 1–9.

Kaslow, F. W. Divorce and divorce therapy. In A. Gurman and D. Kniskern (Eds.). *Handbook of Family Therapy*. New York: Brunner/Mazel, 1981.

Kaslow, F. W. Stages and techniques in divorce therapy. In P. Keller and L. Ritt (Eds.), *Innovations in Clinical Practice: A Sourcebook, Volume II*. Sarasota, Fla.: Professional Resource Exchange, 1983.

Kaslow, F. W. and Friedman, J. Utilization of family photos and movies in family therapy. *Journal of Marital and Family Therapy*, 1977, 3, (1), 19–25.

Langs, R. (Ed.). *Classics in psychoanalytic technique*. New York: Jason Aronson, 1981.

Napier, A. and Whitaker, C. *The family crucible*. New York: Harper and Row, 1978.

Nichols, W. Personal psychotherapy for marital therapists. *Family Coordinator*. April 1968, 17, (2), 83–88.

Williamson, D. S. New life at the graveyard: A method of therapy for individuation from a dead former parent. *Journal of Marital and Family Counseling*, 1978, 4, 93–101.

Williamson, D. S. Personal authority via termination of the intergenerational hierarchical boundary: A 'new' stage in the family life cycle. *Journal of Marital and Family Therapy*, 1981, 7, 441–452.

Notes

1. Comments made by Haley at a workshop for Supervisors of Family Therapy at the Philadelphia Child Guidance Clinic in 1976.

EDITOR'S COMMENTARY

Therapist Self-Disclosure in the Presence of His or Her Significant Others

Often therapists have spent years being introspective about who they are, how they got to be that way, and what is the meaning of life. This introspective quality, combined with rescue fantasies and, sometimes, the need for structured interpersonal relationships that allow safe contact, can be conducive to entering individual therapy and/or a graduate or professional program for would-be therapists. In their personal therapy, as in some classes and supervisory sessions, a high premium is placed on self-revelation and exploration and the development of self-awareness and insight.

Later, much of the acquired ability in self-disclosure may become submerged as the therapist role generally requires listening and responding to the outpourings of patients and not sharing, as a friend might do, one's similar experiences or diverting attention to one's own current problems. (Some exceptions to this are in encounter and sensitivity groups, in which the therapist role shifts to being that of leader/facilitator, and in some family therapy sessions, in which the therapist might purposefully share vignettes about his or her family that he or she deems relevant and helpful.)

When the therapist enters treatment in conjunction with his or her family, self-disclosure is again necessary. One's feelings, perceptions, wishes, goals, frustrations, pent-up anger, disappointments, alliances are all important aspects of the currency within the therapeutic exchange. The therapist member of the family may be quite skilled in manipulating sessions and may know when to talk and when not to talk to elicit certain responses. He may think he's been through sufficient and significant treatment before and that it's the others who need it, so he should sit back. Or risking self-disclosure may be much more difficult as the need to perceive himself and have others view him as healthy and as a good spouse or parent can impede genuine communication. He knows the Pandora's Box that therapy can unlock, and may not wish to have a potentially cataclysmic storm unleashed. Being in the patient role in the here and now may be dreadfully painful and ego dystonic.

Treating other therapists and their families necessitates consummate patience with this possible resistance in addition to an awareness of the other idiosyncratic themes alluded to in the preceding chapter. Once this is mastered, treating other therapists and their families is a special challenge and privilege.

6

Divorce Mediation for Therapists and Their Spouses

William G. Neville, ED.D.

Sometimes marriages end in divorce, and sometimes even a therapist's marriage may end in divorce. This chapter examines some of the ways that therapists and their spouses are involved with the phenomenon of divorce, professionally and personally, and ways they may help their clients and themselves when divorce is imminent. It begins with the least threatening philosophical notions about divorce, moves to the more complex and troublesome area about client couples choosing to get a divorce, and then finally considers the most important area—the therapist's own divorce.

Throughout this chapter I *assume* a position of divorce via mediation. At this point, the reader may not know what that is; however, by the end of the chapter you will probably understand why I assume that when today's therapist thinks of the word "divorce," he or she is likely to think of "mediation."

SOME THOUGHTS ABOUT DIVORCE

For years therapists have taken the position that one of the signs of a functional relationship is its elasticity, its ability to change and be flexible as new demands and stresses come along. The O'Neills wrote nearly ten years ago of the need for *Shifting Gears* (O'Neill & O'Neill, 1974)—the ability of a relationship to be open to the needs of each person in that relationship. Gettleman and Markowitz, in the *Courage to Divorce* (1974), present divorce as a growth phenomenon which, in view of societal pressure to stay in one's rut, calls for real courage to move toward a more viable way of relating. Krantzler (1973) advanced a similar notion in *Creative Divorce* that divorce can provide an opportunity for new understandings of self and hence a new and more real personal presence in relationships. Currently, Carl Whitaker (1981) teaches that keeping the roles in the family flexible and passing them around to different family members, even on a daily basis, is important in assuring that people do not get stuck in positions. Sidney Jourard (1974), in one of his last public addresses, presented the notion that marriage is for the *dynamic* of life rather than the chronological longevity of life, and there is a consequent need for marital partners to develop the skills and abilities to *restructure* their marital relationship to make it viable. During recent years there has been a shift from thinking of divorce as an *ending* to considering it an opportunity for new beginnings for the family, even if not for the marriage.

Divorce is now being seen as a restructuring time rather than an ending, when the family is going through the process of rearranging relationships, responsibilities, and commitments so that its members may individually and collectively get on with the business of living their lives in the most authentic way, given the new circumstances. Fathers will still be fathers, mothers will still be mothers, the children need both and are important to both. Money still passes from hand to hand, feelings still go on, responsibilities are still present, and commitments still exist but "the way we thought it was supposed to be" will evolve into new forms that may be more freeing and responsive than the old positions permitted. Whitaker (1981) has said that he is not sure that anybody ever really gets a divorce. O. J. Coogler, the founder of structured divorce mediation, saw divorce as a restructuring that could open new doors of opportunity for the family rather than as the ending of the family (1974). Morton and Bernice Hunt (1977) and Gettleman and Markowitz (1974) all clearly expound the view that whereas formerly divorce was commonly viewed as a failure, it has now come to be regarded as a creative solution to a problem.

This is not to say that as therapists we should encourage married couples to divorce. But it is to say that as therapists we would be well advised to see divorce as a legitimate alternative to a conflicted marriage, and that it is not a put-down of therapists, nor of therapy, nor of the couple if they choose to divorce. As therapists, we need to examine our own values and belief systems to see clearly what assumptions we hold about life and health, relationships and families, marriage and divorce. Does divorce mean "failure" for the therapist and/or the couple? If indeed it is not a failure, or even "not necessarily" a failure, then how can therapists help people to examine and use this option to accomplish this particular restructuring in the most effective way?

Professionals who work in the area of stress report that what happens to a person is not as important as what one makes of the occurrence (Selye, 1956). If divorce is seen as bad, then the whole divorce process will be bad. If people blame each other for their own feelings and predicament, they will then probably be angry and resentful and constantly attacking and trying to change each other. If, however, they own up to their feelings and accept responsibility for their life, then it is highly likely that they will part with respect and will respond positively to opportunities to be cooperative. The interpretation we give to the circumstances of our life is of our own choosing, and the choice we make will impact heavily, either positively or negatively, on our children.

Those who have worked closely with people who are dissolving their marriages are very clear that the key issue is not *whether* a couple divorces but rather *how* they accomplish that shift. Some couples go at their divorce as though they were combatants in a cock fight, and the carnage may—in fact, *will* probably—continue for years. Some attorneys fan the fires of the fight and escalate the "legal" destruction of people who once loved each other dearly and still care deeply about their children.[1]

This escalation of the competitive battle is frequently done "in the best interest of the child." All indications are, however, that the best interest of the child is served by a process that escalates not the conflict and competitiveness but the cooperation and communication of the parents. The children are not getting a divorce from their parents, nor are the parents divorcing their children. Roman and Haddad (1974), in *The Disposable Parent: The Case for Joint Custody*, cite a New York-based study of over 2,000 children in which it was clearly shown that "the major factor affecting the children's happiness is the relationship between the parents" (p. 69) and that studies consistently showed that "those children who fared best after the divorce were those who were free to develop loving and full relationships with *both* parents" (p. 71).

Yet it has been estimated that over 100,000 children are kidnapped each year by angry parents (Wiegner, 1979). Conversely, research on mediation (Parker, 1980) has documented that over 90 percent of the mediated clients were satisfied with their settlements and over 93 percent were satisfied with their custody and visitation rights. It was further noted in this Atlanta-based study that most of the mediated couples spoke caringly of their former spouses, whereas the adversarial clients, *if they spoke of their former spouses at all,* tended to do so with hostility and bitterness.

In the public sector, judges are referring couples who are arguing about the provisions of the divorce agreement for court-based mediation services that usually entail dealing with child custody and visitation issues. In the private sector, some couples decide to mediate rather than litigate all aspects of their divorce—custody, visitation, and division of assets. They want to avoid becoming adversaries and prefer seeking a cooperative pathway to marital dissolution.

There is an increasing number of couples who have restructured their relationships in most creative, caring, and cooperative ways. Although such a reconstituted family is different from what it was, the children often wind up getting the best of both parents and a new sense of responding to life creatively when life does not go the way they want it to go. Instead of being bitter and hostile, these children will probably grow up to be happy, well-adjusted people who flow freely back and forth between parents who care about and respect each other for who they are and who do not continue to resent who they are not. So the *way,* or the *how,* of the divorce, rather than the fact of divorce per se, seems to be the key variable.

People who work in the areas of conflict resolution have shown clearly that *cooperative problem solving* approaches will yield quite different results from *competitive problem solving* approaches (Deutsch, 1973). The competitive approach is basically what we have in our adversarial system. It is a win-lose proposition, and nobody likes to be a loser. So, the fight is usually over what we *don't* want (that is, being a loser) rather than over what we do want (that is, a relationship of marriage *or* divorce that will work). This competitive approach is much like a poker game, in which one plays one's cards close to the vest, deceiving, distorting, hiding, and the winner takes all (except, that is, what gets paid to the attorneys)!

The cooperative approach is a win-win approach, and one

plays with all the cards face up in *full disclosure*. Information is shared, and people find their own interests being served by making sure the other party's needs are taken care of, too—at least to the same extent as their own. The cooperative approach fosters responsibility rather than blame, communication rather than isolation, creativity rather than stagnation, and flexibility rather than rigidity. Clearly, the cooperative approach is better for human beings who live in a democratic society, yet our country seems to be sowing the seeds of its own destruction by encouraging the competitive approach at nearly every *level* from womb to tomb. Unless we learn to do cooperative problem solving, the natural results of the competitive approach may well be our demise.[2]

Throughout the history of our country, divorce has been seen as "against public policy" and therefore something to which people could not agree. To get a divorce, one person had to file legal suit against the other, immediately creating a plaintiff-defendant, or adversarial, posture between people who had once chosen to be lifelong partners and who, over the years, had both given to and received from each other; who probably had shared in the creation of children and who had experienced many hurts and disappointments in their unfulfilled expectations of each other and of the relationship. So, at the very time when that couple was most in need of careful, cooperative planning for the future and most in need of shared communication, our legal system, representing societal expectations, was not just urging, it was demanding that this couple become adversaries and competitors over their own children and estate. Property division and support payments were commonly awarded as spoils to the victor, and the loser could then continue to fight by appealing the award, being negligent of the obligations, or just simply leaving the territory. It is no wonder, then, under such a prevailing philosophy, that divorce came to be experienced as destructive and that the results were so devastating to the kind of community and family life our country was espousing. Because of the way divorce was handled, couples with deep, joint emotional histories became bitter enemies, and the "family," instead of becoming the "school of community," became the battleground for the present generation and the "war college" of competitive litigation for the next. Courts are clogged with postdivorce renegotiations, and child support payments are seriously in arrears. Fathers generally pay less than a third of what is due, and over half the fathers do not pay at all (Baldus, 1980). Something about our traditional way of assisting families at this time of transition and rebuilding is not working.

MEDIATION AS AN ALTERNATIVE

In 1974, O. J. Coogler, a retired attorney turned family therapist, who was experiencing the frustration of the adversarial approach to family restructuring, undertook to provide an alternative process that would be more in keeping with what we know today of families and of the resolution of conflict. Coogler developed a process he called "structured mediation in divorce settlement" (Coogler, 1978) and, while this process has since undergone some changes, it is still essentially a cooperative rather than a competitive approach that builds on full disclosure, shared information, and mutually agreed upon decisions.

This approach is still so new that good long-term research results are just beginning to become available. The implication seems to be, however, that when couples are offered the mediation alternative, about 50 percent will choose it and of those who choose it, approximately 80 percent will complete the process, with most of the others saying that even though they did not finish the process, it was still a very beneficial experience for them (Pearson, 1981). Clearly, the cooperative approach of mediation offers families going through divorce the option of responsible restructuring.

HOW THERAPISTS CAN ASSIST
COOPERATIVE PROBLEM SOLVING

The process is so new, however, that many lay people have never heard of mediation. When people are in crisis, the word of the expert they have chosen to shepherd them carries enormous weight. If therapists are knowledgeable about mediation, recommend it to their clients, support their using it, and make good referrals to trained mediators, they will be providing their patient families with the best possible service available at this time. Any written settlement has both a legal and an emotional dimension, and both must be carefully tended to have a "good" settlement—that is, one that works.

Mediation is a new field and new profession that draws upon knowledge and skills from the fields of law and mental health. Just as the mediator does not replace the attorney, neither does he or she replace the therapist during the divorce sequence. The attorney's role is that of a legal information consultant and a drafter of a clear and solid agreement for the couple, and the mediator must be careful not to practice law without a license.

The role of the therapist is to assist the client in interpreting the various parts of the divorce experience. The clients may need therapeutic assistance with moving through the process of grief (including shock, denial, anger, and sadness); developing a good, positive sense of self-worth; discovering a newly individuated sense of identity; updating appropriate social behaviors; completing and turning loose the past; and sharing the excitement of new beginnings and accomplishments.[3] While the mediator may use some of the skills of the therapist in responding to emotional data, *the couple has come to the mediator for a problem-solving task,* and the mediator should refer the couple to their therapist for dealing with such things as anger, grief, or resentment in a constructive way. The mediator may, for example, stop a mediation session if one party is too emotionally upset to make rational decisions. A good approach for the mediator would then be to send the clients back to their therapist before mediation continues. Even the process of deciding whether to divorce or not should be accomplished with the therapist rather than the mediator. But once the decision to divorce has been made, well-intentioned therapists who are poorly informed about the specifics and intricacies of the settlement itself would serve their clients best by referring them to a mediator and letting therapy take an ancillary role for a short while. A competent professional, be he or she therapist, mediator, or attorney, is a well-individuated person—clear about his or her identity and contribution, yet appreciative of the role of others; not into "client stealing" nor so frightened or greedy that the best care is withheld out of fear of losing a client. There are many ways a good therapist can grease the wheels of the mediation process.

One of the first things that a referring therapist can do for the client couple coming into mediation is to assist them to determine clearly what their intentions are and help them to develop a cooperative problem-solving approach to their dissolution and restructuring. Until people are clear about their intentions, they will flounder from one approach to another, looking for what fits their needs at any given moment. It is important that they understand clearly, are aware that mediation means learning to be cooperative, and adopt cooperative problem-solving behavior. They will then do whatever is necessary to accomplish their task. Instead of saying "I'll be cooperative to a point, but I will reserve the final judgment until I see how the whole thing turns out" or "I'll make a little bit of 'full disclosure' and see what happens" or "I'll see how cooperative my spouse will be and then make my judgment about whether this will work for us" people will literally come in *expecting* to cooperate, to be corrected where they get off the track, and to have the process work for them. And it will! Success and failure tend to be self-reinforcing experiences. So it is with mediation. Some people may not have had much experience in operating on the basis of personal responsibility and choice, and would rather blame circumstances, processes, spouses, mediators, and/or therapists. But taking responsibility for their own contribution to their divorce and choosing how they would prefer the mediation to go are enormously important in the results they obtain. The therapist can therefore perform a valuable service for these clients and the mediator by helping the couple become clear about what their intentions are and whether they are going to have a cooperative or competitive divorce!

Therapists also can greatly assist this restructuring process by helping the clients forgive—forgive their spouses and themselves. Forgiveness is not the process of "making the other person be right." In our competitive society, we frequently withhold forgiveness because we have no intention of giving more points to our adversary. The therapist, however, can help the client see that *forgiveness is that process by which the client turns loose the past and in so doing is enabled to get on with life in the present.* Anybody who is not forgiving is continuing to live in the past and is missing out on life in the present. They remain stuck and stymied, frustrated and furious, and will very likely be involved in litigation for a long, long time. It is essential for a healthy divorce and a cooperative problem-solving approach that people learn to turn loose the past, to forgive themselves and their partners for things they did and things they failed to do.

As a person begins to let go of or become extricated from the past, he or she can begin to see more clearly the tasks that lie ahead. The client then can focus appropriately on the anxiety of the unknown future and in so doing often finds that the partner whom they have just forgiven for "what they were not" has suddenly become a willing ally and support, for example, on the responsibilities of raising the children they have in common. Mediation *invites* people to share what they are *willing* to do rather than attempting to command them about what they *have* to do. The cooperative approach of mediation tends to elicit a person's best and most responsible self, and frequently one partner is surprised by the creative expressions of caring that come forth from this apparent competitor. One husband, for example, said to his wife, who was to have custody of their children, that he would be glad to share "sick time" with her since they both worked. There was no reason that she should always take time off from her work to be with the children when they were sick just because she had custody; he would be willing to share "sick time" with her on a fifty-fifty basis.

Another task for which the therapist is most appropriately trained is that of helping the client with the cognitive part of the restructuring process of divorce. How do you let go of your belief in "happily ever after"? When the world has not gone the way you expected it to, dealing with the cognitive dissonance that results becomes very important, yet it is frequently pushed aside for more immediate or seemingly more important matters. This is a problem that will continue to surface for the client throughout the year and a "good" therapist will stay in touch with the client during mediation and in the year that follows to assist at those points. Holidays, for example, evoke nostalgia and memories of "the way it used to be." This may resurface from time to time over a period of several years. The mediation process enables people to experience personal confirmation more easily and thereby tends to reduce the time needed to make a successful transition. A skillful therapist can reenforce both the mediation process and the successful transition of the client.

Some therapists have found a "divorce ceremony" a helpful tool. At a time when our society has no ritual to mark or acknowledge this change in status and when no one knows quite what to say, reading such a ceremony with a couple can be very healing. The whole process of attaining closure to a relationship means attending to the many aspects that are still unfinished, and the symbolic elements of a ritual may provide a context for the family to accomplish this. The best ceremony I have seen was written by Henry Close, a pastoral counselor and family therapist in Ft. Lauderdale, Florida (1977). The Methodist church and the Jewish faith both have ceremonies in their prayer books, but a good ceremony is hard to find in many faiths, and nondenominational ceremonies are a rarity. It should avoid the gimmicky and speak sensitively to the deepest emotions of the heart. (See Kaslow, 1981, for one such ceremony.)

THE BEST INTEREST OF THE CHILD

A question that frequently comes up is "What is in the best interest of the child?" I believe we would all agree that a good, healthy, functional family is in the best interest of the child. Given the restructuring through divorce, however, it would seem that the child's best interest entails seeing the parents acting in a cooperative problem-solving mode rather than acting out their bitterness and frustration in a competitive way. Children grow up in all sorts, sizes, and shapes of family life. Wallerstein and Kelly (1975) have carefully documented the different response patterns based on children's ages. Gardner (1970) has emphasized the need for honesty and information with children. Ricci (1981), Lewis (1980), Kaslow (1981) and others have also added to the multiple dimensions of divorce and remarriage. Yet, through it all, the key variable in the well-being of the child seems to be the well-being of the adults. So, rather than getting yet another attorney to represent "the best interest of the child" and thereby even further fragmenting the family, it makes sense for therapists, attorneys, and mediators to work together to support the couple in their best efforts of communication, cooperation, caring, creativity, closure, and consensus.

PERSONAL USE OF MEDIATION
BY THE THERAPIST

Sometimes divorce happens for therapists. And when it does, the therapist has his or her own professional training and occupational hazards to contend with. The therapist may be hit with an acute sense of personal failure, especially if he or she has been helpful to others in sorting out and clarifying their couple relationship. When this becomes a therapist's predicament, he or she should do what we teach—stay with the feelings and realize how frequently they want to hide and distort the way it is. We tend to forget that therapists are first of all *people*—and our working with others will be helpful to the extent that we are willing to be authentic with our clients. When one looks at the different approaches of, say, Rogers (1961), Skinner (1938), and Perls (1973), what is revealed are the differences of each of those *people* being expressed in ways that are authentic for them; but for Fritz to try to be a little Carl would simply not work. It is easy to want to maintain an image one has built up, and to the extent that we are successful at image building, we are also successful at hiding our humanity. "How can I maintain my image in front of you, my colleague, when you see what a failure I am with my own family?"

Using mediation services is an opportunity to put into practice the principles of mental health we have been espousing. It is important for therapists to remember that as *people* we, too, have emotions and needs; we, too, have sadness and grief; we, too, experience feelings of failure and aloneness; we, too, need to give and receive forgiveness; and we, too, desire closure. And we need to remember in mediation that it is all right for us not to have all the answers, and it's permissible to get angry and "lose our cool." It is also acceptable to be scared and keep sabotaging our intention to be cooperative. It is legitimate to be human.

Mediation really gets embarrassing when we see our spouse coming through with more clear, sure, and cooperative behavior than we: "After all, I'm the one with all the training in relationships. Self-disclosure and the sharing of feelings is the name of my game. . . ." Pogo says, "We have met the enemy, and he is us!" We do have occupational hazards in the helping professions; we must acknowledge them and be open to learning—not only from our colleagues but also from those whom we may consider least likely to teach us anything: our spouses.

Our professional training tends to militate against our being good clients for mediation in that we are too frequently taught to observe the other person's behavior and label it. For example, someone else is being "resistant" when they don't see it our way. In mediation, we are exposed to the reality that many of our labels become coverups for our own unwillingness to be authentic. And when we have diagnosed our own family, it is particularly difficult to be open to a second opinion.

Have we been taught to understand others' feelings and be so sensitive to their needs that *we* don't know how to be assertive and count *ourselves* in? People get *so* cooperative in mediation that in a traditional family where the husband works away from home and the wife works within the home, husbands tend to over-give and wives tend to under-ask. (If there is a pitfall to mediation, this is it.) Mediation is basically a problem-solving task, yet trained and experienced therapists are frequently so concerned with listening and hearing that they may find themselves virtually incapable of making decisions, especially if they seem a little bit selfish when they are the clients. It is easy for the therapist-client in mediation to feel such a keen sense of guilt that he or she will go to virtually any lengths to atone for his or her past failures. Since we are frequently the ones who "mediate the forgiveness" in society, we may have an overly difficult time receiving it.

Mediation, however, calls for one to come down from the therapist's pedestal and be equal, to ask for what is wanted, and to negotiate for what is to be gotten. One piece of research that is under way seems to be indicating a lack of success in mediation for the "educated" (Thoennes, 1982). Could this mean that education can work both ways and that while it can provide more opportunities, it can also indicate more ways to hide? I remember a presentation that Sidney Jourard (1962) made to a group of ministers on being authentic, and the entire talk, which was very short, seems appropriate for inclusion here. "Well," he said, "we're all phonies. And it seems to me that it is simply a question of whether you are willing to be a real phony or whether you are going to be a phony phony."

TRAINING

Mediation is a first cousin of therapy. But then it is also a first cousin of the practice of law. And it is neither therapy nor law. Mediation is mediation. It is one person assisting two others to find a mutually agreeable solution to the problems inherent in marital dissolution. There may be a tendency for some therapists to want to plunge in to become mediators—especially if their practice of therapy is not going all that well. They may want to become all things to all people. I caution therapists about attempting to do mediation without first having some good basic training in the field. There are a number of people and groups offering training in mediation; some have lots of experience and some have virtually none. The field is gradually developing standardized training and certification procedures. Until these are adopted, I am concerned lest therapists who are not trained as mediators offer their services to the public as such, only to have certain errors and omissions occur that embarrass the whole field of mediation and short-change the clients. Mediation is a splendid process, and it works for many participants, but because it is still in a fledgling stage, it is subjected to very careful scrutiny. The adversarial approach may create far more havoc in domestic relations than mediation ever could or would, but since it is the time-honored approach, its practitioners seldom get more than a verbal admonition from the bar or the bench for any shortcomings on their part.

Because of the close scrutiny of mediation, however, any miscue on the part of a mediator can have serious repercussions for the whole movement. Therefore, if a therapist is doing "divorce counseling," it should not be labeled "mediation"; and a therapist, who is doing or wants to be doing mediation should first take one of the basic five-day training programs. It will not equip a novice mediator completely; in fact, it will barely scratch the surface, but this is the minimum beginning preparation that is acceptable.

Generally, people going into mediation training should have at least a master's degree in one of the helping professions. During this prior learning they have covered at least the minimal elements of sensitivity training, communication skills, growth and development, life cycle issues, and it is to be hoped, some introspective work in looking at their own personality dynamics.

If an attorney wants to become a mediator, the same basic five-day training would be an appropriate beginning. Remember that although mediation is a first cousin to the practice of law, it is *not* the practice of law. It involves a whole range of knowledge of behavior, motivation, learning, family and interpersonal dynamics, skills, and even a theology that would very likely be new to an attorney. Just as a therapist may be wise to take some legal courses in family law, taxation, and family finance, an attorney would be well advised to take some training in family systems, sensitivity training, and communications skills, death and dying, and personality development.

Since an attorney may be used directly in the mediation process as a legal information consultant, it may be redundant to seek to be the mediator, since then yet another attorney would be

116

PSYCHOTHERAPY WITH PSYCHOTHERAPISTS

needed as the information consultant and to draft the agreement in legal form. In any case, the attorney-mediator and therapist-mediator would need to be quite clear about their roles at any particular time. The skills, training, and practice of mediation are similar to and different from both therapy and law.

I believe that the actual *effectiveness* of the mediator, however, is not a matter of his or her training but of the "gifts" with which that particular person is endowed. Some may be trained to be teachers and still not be effective as a teacher; some may be trained as physicians and still not be effective in healing. In all of our interpersonal professions, the effectiveness of that particular professional is largely a matter of who that *person* is and how he or she expresses personhood through a particular professional stance. We are our own best tool and must learn what that tool does most effectively. Each mediator should manifest what he or she purports to do in how it is done. The field of mediation should be based and built on the principles of cooperative problem solving, and any competitiveness, whether in training or in the development of the field, has no place in this movement. Anything built on such competitiveness will not last.

CONCLUSION

Divorce is a phenomenon of our day. How divorce is handled will make a difference, literally, for generations yet unborn. Mediation is a cooperative approach to domestic problem solving, and research shows that when this option is made available to the public, the majority choose it and find it helpful (Pearson, 1982).

The family is frequently referred to as "the school of community." A community implies both communication and cooperation. Divorce mediation is the process of assisting the family to continue to fulfill this function even as it seems precariously close to losing it. Cooperative problem solving is participatory democracy, and divorce mediation for therapists is the opportunity for us as therapists to expand our beliefs, to rediscover ourselves, and to offer a more peaceful world to our grandchildren.

References

Baldus, A. Book Review, 78 *Michigan Law Review* 750, 1980. (Reviewing David L. Chambers, *Making fathers pay: The enforcement of child support,* 1979.)

Close, H. A service of divorce. *Pilgrimage,* Spring, 1977, 5, (1).

Coogler, O. J. Personal conversations, Nov. 1974.

Coogler, O. J. *Structured mediation in divorce settlement.* Lexington, Ma.: D.C. Heath, 1978.

Deutsch, M. *The resolution of conflict.* New Haven: Yale University Press, 1973.

Etheridge, J. Personal conversation, Emory Law School, Atlanta, Ga., March 1983.

Gardner, R. *The boys and girls book about divorce.* New York: Bantam, 1970.

Gettlemen, S., & Markowitz, J. *The courage to divorce.* New York: Simon and Schuster, 1974.

Hunt, M., & Hunt, B. *The divorce experience.* New York: McGraw-Hill, 1977.

Jampolsky, G. G. *Love is letting go of fear.* Millbrae, Ca.: Celestial Arts, 1979.

Jourard, S. Presbyterian ministers retreat at Starke, Fl., 1962.

Jourard, S. AAMFT meeting, St. Louis, Mo., Nov. 1974.

Kaslow, F. Divorce and divorce therapy. In A. Gurman & D. Kniskern *Handbook of Family Therapy.* New York: Brunner/Mazel, 1981.

Kessler, S. *The American way of divorce: Prescription for change.* Chicago: Nelson Hall, 1975.

Krantzler, M. *Creative divorce.* New York: Signet, 1973.

Lewis, H. C. *All about families the second time around.* Atlanta, Ga.: Peachtree Publishers, 1980.

O'Neill, N., & O'Neill, G. *Shifting gears.* New York: Avon Books, 1974.

Parker, A. A comparison of divorce mediation versus lawyer adversary processes and the relationship to marital separation factors. (Doctoral dissertation, University of North Carolina, 1980).

Pearson, J. & Thoennes, N. The mediation and adjudication of divorce disputes: Some costs and benefits. *Family Advocate.* January 1982, 4, (3).

Perls, F. S. *The Gestalt approach.* Palo Alto: Science and Behavior Books, 1973.

Ricci, I. *Mom's house, Dad's house.* New York: Macmillan, 1981.

Rogers, C. *On becoming a person.* Boston: Houghton Mifflin, 1961.

Roman, M., & Haddad, W. *The disposable parent: The case for joint custody.* New York: Penguin, 1974.

Selye, H. *The stress of life.* New York: McGraw-Hill, 1956.

Shaffer, T. Lawyers, counselors, and counselors at law, *American Bar Association Journal* July 1975, 61.

Skinner, B. B. *The behavior of organisms.* New York: Appleton-Century-Crofts, 1938.

Thoennes, N. Personal conversation, AAMFT meeting, Dallas, Texas, Nov. 1982.

Wallerstein, J., & Kelly, J. Experiences of the pre-school child. *Journal of the American Academy of Child Psychiatry*, 1975, *14*, 600–616.

Whitaker, C. Annual meeting of Georgia Marriage and Family Therapists, Jekyll Island, Ga. April 1981.

Wiegner, K. The high cost of leaving, *Forbes*, February 19, 1979.

Notes

1. There are three elements that go into the making of an attorney that cause this negative approach to domestic dispute resolution:

a. Historically, our legal system has come from English law, which sought to establish guilt and innocence and to lay blame for the "failure" of the marriage. Compare this, for example, with the Japanese system, in which the couple simply goes before the magistrate and signs the appropriate document saying that they now choose to divorce—no legal suit, no blame, yet Japan's divorce rate is about one-third that of the United States.

b. The adversarial approach is based on the assumption that where the two litigants are represented by advocates (presumed to be equal in power but, in fact, with wide variations of power and skill) who pull out all stops and give no quarter, truth, or a close approximation of it, will emerge. This approach assumes that though at times the process may be destructive, the responsibility for the carnage lies with the "bad" party who caused the divorce. The attorney's job is to control aggression by obtaining a judgment in his or her client's favor as swiftly and totally as possible (Shaffer, 1975). This pits spouses against each other in an adversarial battle, missing totally, for example, the concept of the family-as-client. It promotes winners and losers rather than the restructuring of a family.

c. An attorney's training teaches him or her *not* to pay attention to feelings, but to deal only with what the law says (Etheridge, 1983). Feelings are viewed as subjective, changing, and individual, whereas the law deals with behavior—concrete, specific, and objective. The failure to see the connection between these two results in legal decisions being rendered that in fact do *not* settle the problem because they have not dealt with that which is most personal—the meaning to the individuals of their behavior and relationship.

2. Quite literally, the future continuance or extinction of the human race may depend on how quickly we decide to cooperatively deescalate the insanity of the nuclear arms competition, which in itself is a natural result of a world run by competitive family patterns. There is a growing interest in

the development of a National Peace Academy, which would be committed to these same cooperative problem solving approaches at the international level (National Peace Academy Campaign, Suite 409, 110 Maryland Ave., N.E., Washington, D.C. 20002).

3. There are many good books that can be quite helpful in these areas. Three I frequently consult are: Sheila Kessler's *The American Way of Divorce* (1975), Mel Krantzler's *Creative Divorce* (1973), and Gerry Jampolsky's *Love Is Letting Go of Fear* (1979).

EDITOR'S COMMENTARY

Mediation: A New Approach to a Painful Parting Process

In this chapter, Neville is probably the first one to tackle the knotty problem of mediating a therapist's divorce. Since he is an ordained and practicing clergyman, a trained and well-respected marital therapist, and one of the earliest and best recognized mediators, his contribution was requested because he brings an unusually fine combination of attributes to the task.

Because the theory and technique of divorce mediation are in existence less than a decade, and he assumes that some of our readers might not be familiar with this legitimate alternative method of marital dissolution, Neville begins the chapter with an overview of the major premises of mediation. He writes from the perspective of one who sees divorce as a potentially creative way to end a conflicted, incompatible marriage and highlights the opportunities for growth it affords. With perceptive wisdom he points out that we all ultimately choose both "the interpretation we give to the circumstances of our life," and how we accomplish the shifts that are imperative around marker events. It is how these transitions are made and the interpretation, rather than the actual occurrence, of the event (in this instance, the divorce) that have the greatest impact on the childrens' reactions and state of well-being.

Neville highlights the key precepts of mediation, such as *empowerment* to maximize one's own participation in the decision-making process inherent in divorce and the establishment of a *cooperative* attitude and atmosphere focusing on the best interest of each member of the family. This style and philosophy is in distinct contrast to the competitive struggle mandated by a litigated divorce. The judicial system is predicated on the assumption that in a dispute between two parties one is guilty and so must pay a penalty and the other is innocent and injured and is therefore due recompense. Mediation facilitates recognition of and even concern for the participants' needs in life and sets the groundwork for moving into the present and future and not remaining inextricably stuck in the past.

Mediation's philosophy that divorce is not an ending of a family but rather a *restructuring* of family relationships, alignments, and power distribution concurs with the best current thinking regarding the post-divorce family as articulated by Sager and his colleagues in *Treating the Remarried Family* (Sager et al., 1983). The single most compelling fact is that the children are not divorcing their parents, nor are the adults severing their parental ties with the children. Thus, as the spousal bond is dissolved, new arrangements for being separated parents in a joint venture need to be forged sensibly. And the two parties, in evolving their own agreement, are likely to be more invested in keeping it or altering it jointly as the passage of time necessitates modifications.

Essential to the successful culmination of the mediation process are: full self-disclosure of all financial assets, authenticity, and integrity in negotiations. The process encourages the participants' optimism about the future through its enhancement of self-esteem and sense of competence in an ability to work out an agreement and reshape their lives. Thus, it would seem natural that therapists, who seek to treat others as humanely as possible and who prefer constructive rather than destructive interpersonal and transactional relationships, would gravitate toward mediation if they have decided to end their marital union. The philosophic assumptions and premises of mediation are congruent with those of all schools of therapy, and should be much more syntonic with the personal value system of most therapists than are the principles that undergird the adversarial divorce process.

Thus, we felt that inclusion of this chapter in a book on *Psychotherapy with Psychotherapists* was a logical extension of the continuum of marriage, family, and divorce therapy for and with this special professional population and their significant others. Perhaps it may illuminate a much more acceptable passageway to some who have long avoided seeking a divorce because of their aversion to the customary procedures.

References

Sager, C. J., Brown, H. S., Crohn, H., Engel, T., Rodstein, E., & Walker, L. *Treating the remarried family.* N.Y.: Brunner/Mazel, 1983.

7

Group Psychotherapy for Group Therapists

Erich Coché, PH.D.

After conducting psychotherapy groups in one's own personal style, a therapist is confronted by three main dangers. Although most therapists are aware of these to some degree and have developed their own ways of dealing with them, they are still worth noting because of their potential detrimental effects on therapy groups.[1] This chapter advocates the use of a therapy group for therapists as a method of preventing or coping with the following dangers:

1. With increasing years of experience, many therapists begin to nurture the belief that they have already found the answers to all the problems a group can possibly present. Responding to those problems, they can reach back into their fund of accumulated experience and apply those techniques that have served them well in past years. This, however, causes some therapists to become blasé and stereotypic in their response patterns.
2. Many experienced therapists tend to forget how anxiety arousing a group can be to a participant, how hard it is sometimes to disclose personally troublesome material to a group of peers, and how frightening situations can be as, for instance, the first session, when one is not "in the driver's seat." A group for therapists can refresh those memories and give the therapist a renewed understanding of the feelings of the participants.
3. As time goes on, group therapists tend to become less aware of their own power in a group. I have seen professionals ascribe enormous powers to someone who by all other indicators was their peer, but was now treated as more than that because he or

she was assigned the group leader role. Groups tend to invest almost mystical powers in their leaders. Thus, a group magnifies the impact of a leader's utterances for better or worse. There is much potential for healing in such a powerful position, but there is as much seduction for abuse and even more potential for harmful effects if the leader either is unaware of this power or denies its existence. Participation in a group for advanced therapists can reinforce the lesson the therapist needs to keep in mind if power is to be used to the advantage of the patient seeking help.

Continuing education is not limited to cognitive subject matter but can also apply to affective-experiential learning. Some therapists' blind spots develop long after their training, and intermittent intensive group experiences can provide refreshing new impulses for introspection and personal change, which in turn have a salutory effect on the therapist's work. Professionals who have participated in the psychodynamic process groups at the annual institutes of the American Group Psychotherapy Association have repeatedly expressed how profoundly they have been affected by these groups (Coché, Dies, & Albrecht, 1982). Here, too, the learning acquired was seen not only as beneficial to one's work with clients, but also as personally meaningful and growth producing.

In this chapter, I discuss first the rationales that have been advanced in favor of group psychotherapy for psychotherapists. The central section discusses the issues, problems, and choices inherent in the conduct of groups for group therapists. Finally, there is some discussion of the application of concepts of this chapter to therapy groups for beginning group therapists.

RATIONALES FOR THERAPY GROUPS
FOR THERAPISTS

Being in the Patient Role

As already mentioned, participation in a therapy group gives the group therapist first-hand knowledge of some of the anxieties, joys, and frustrations that any group therapy patient experiences. Patients are naturally anxious when a group works out its leadership problems. Going through such group events and feeling the pangs of anxiety very directly provides healthy reminders that can enhance the degree and the accuracy of a group therapist's empathy upon return to the groups he or she is leading.

Isomorphism

Group therapy supervisors who conduct training groups for students or for advanced therapists are frequently surprised by the regularity with which similar issues appear both in the supervisory groups and in the groups their candidates are leading. A principle of isomorphism is often invoked, but is frequently treated as if it were something mysterious and inexplicable. On reflection, however, it becomes rather simple and perfectly logical that this phenomenon should occur. First of all, groups are groups. They proceed with a reasonable degree of regularity from one developmental stage to another, as has been described by many authors (Thelen, 1954; Bennis & Shepard, 1956; Beck, 1981; Beck & Peters, 1981). Regardless of the particular schema one follows, it is likely that very similar types of occurrences develop, depending on the stage a group is in.

Secondly, it is likely that a therapist who leads a group has certain personal and interpersonal issues that will be evoked in some form in the groups he or she is leading as well as the one he or she is participating in. For example, group therapists who have unresolved authority conflicts are likely to focus excessively on this issue in the groups they lead. It is equally likely that they will make this a major issue in the groups in which they participate. Whatever the core conflict may be (such as authority, dependency, or intimacy), it usually does not matter what side of the drama one is on. I have seen therapists switch back and forth in the roles of rebel and dictator from one group to the other, spending considerable amounts of time on the activity, and blatantly seducing other members of either group into playing the contrapuntal role.

Common Therapeutic Advantages

If the group for therapists is indeed a psychotherapy group (as opposed to a seminar), it is likely also to have all the therapeutic elements of any psychotherapy group: among other benefits, it provides its patients with feedback on their behaviors and can help in removing blind spots and in improving communications skills. Most of all, such a therapy group can help its participants to work out some of their own problems that otherwise might be foisted onto their present or future clients. In this regard, group therapy has a distinct advantage over individual therapy because it allows the therapist, the other group members, and the leader of the group to observe the behavior of the member in a group situation.

ISSUES IN THE CONDUCT OF GROUP THERAPY FOR GROUP THERAPISTS

Some practical and theoretical issues must be confronted when one conducts group therapy for psychotherapists. In generating this list of issues, and in formulating some of the answers, I am relying mostly on my personal experiences gathered by participating in and leading such groups.[2]

The following sections address many problems to be faced when designing a group therapeutic experience for therapists. The problems have been organized into three major clusters:

1. Issues that create or enhance resistance among the participants,
2. Issues of format and design that should be addressed before starting the group,
3. Problems typical of all therapy groups, but perhaps exacerbated in groups designed for therapists.

RESISTANCE

Resistance is the central problem for the leader and the group (I. Berger, 1969). Being in a group is always somewhat anxiety arousing, and self-disclosure is difficult for most people under normal circumstances. However, when this is happening to an already established professional within the framework of a therapeutic group, it is likely to create formidable barriers to self-exploration. Resistance in such a group stems from many sources, some of which are elucidated later in this chapter. Overcoming resistance is frequently the overriding goal and ultimate sign of success for this type of group.

Resistance can take many forms, the most frequent and obvious ones being prolonged silences, excessive intellectualization, lateness, absences, or over-talkativeness. More subtle forms of resistance, like the squelching of enthusiasm of more active members, can often go unnoticed for quite a while, but once detected and discussed are often more easily overcome than the more dramatic symptoms.

A Group of Therapists

Since groups of group therapists consist of mental health professionals, there is a constant danger that everyone in the group will want to be the therapist, and no one will want to play the patient role. These groups can develop superb levels of sophistication in making interpretations for one another, but have trouble finding volunteers to be the recipients of their ministrations. Thus, as Yalom (1975) pointed out, intellectualization is likely to be so commonplace as to make true therapeutic work extremely difficult. It is also quite likely that there will be at least two or three members in the group who will finally become very tired of the constant intellectualization and will take considerable interpersonal risk in order to move the group forward. In this sense, the therapist in the patient role can be both a source of resistance and a force to overcome it.

Institutional Embeddedness

Another set of problems arises out of the fact that many groups for therapists are assembled from within an institution. Frequently the group is part of a special experience organized for members of the staff. The members' familiarity with each other and the conflict created by the multiple role relationships of being colleague and co-trainee can increase resistance considerably, as illustrated by examples below.

Confidentiality

In most psychotherapy groups, members are understandably concerned that their self-disclosures remain confidential. This becomes even more an issue when the members are also working with one another and with colleagues who do not belong to the group. Concerns about confidentiality frequently determine the content of the first few sessions. Setting rules in this regard may become the first decision-making activity within a new group, and dependency issues can come to a head at this juncture when the group demands that the leader establish clear standards from the outset, and the leader responds by telling the group that it should solve this problem itself and create its own norms and regulations. Thus, many groups for therapists "get going" around the confidentiality issue. Usually, they find a satisfactory solution, but until they do, and if they do not, they can become so concerned over possible violations of confidentiality that this issue itself becomes a major point of resistance and can severely hamper the process of the group.

Hierarchical Structure

It is not uncommon for groups of therapists to comprise members of different levels within the organizational hierarchy of their institution. This too can become a point of resistance; superiors may feel greatly inhibited in front of the people who work for them; the latter, in turn, may resist involvement because they are afraid to look foolish or weak in the eyes of their superiors. Occasionally, the lower-ranking members will become hyperexpressive, exerting excessive amounts of energy in order to impress their bosses. Where such phenomena occur, they need to be dealt with. Given a skillful leader and a modicum of trust within the group these problems can be overcome and lead to better understanding between the participants.

Of course, hierarchy and institution-related problems can be avoided altogether if group therapists choose to participate in stranger groups convened outside of their organization.

FORMAT CHOICES

The person who organizes a therapeutic experience for group therapists is well advised to consider a number of choices carefully before beginning. Owing to prior experiences, he or she may have a preference for a certain way of conducting such a group, but the many complex issues that tend to arise frequently require differentiated, thoughtful answers for which there may be no prior models. In this section, some choices are detailed.

Group Therapists Only or a Mixed Group

Seeking a group experience outside of one's own institution and circle of acquaintances prevents many of the problems just mentioned. Furthermore, one needs to ask whether the therapy experience is likely to be more genuine and more therapeutic if the therapist is a member of a group of therapists, or in a group with other patients who are not mental health professionals. Certainly there is less likelihood that the kind of intellectualization mentioned earlier will develop in the latter type of group. However, there is a danger that fellow group members may see the mental health professional as another therapist and treat him or her accordingly. Conversely, the professional who is a patient in such a group may enjoy the special status. Most groups, fortunately, only show such preferential treatment for a brief time. After that, they are likely to insist that the therapist-patient become a fellow patient regardless of his or her status in the "outside world". As Dies has pointed out (1983), another problem arises if the therapist who participates in a genuine group has no actual symptoms—in contrast to the rest of the group members. This is likely to further enhance his or her special role.

At the point at which the group begins to work on its leadership and authority problems, the mental health professional who is a patient in a group with lay people is likely to take on a special role. He or she may become a substitute for the leader and be attacked merely because the group is not quite ready to attack the group leader, but does want to begin working on the authority issues with which they need to deal. It is up to the leader to be cognizant of this development and to prevent such substitute whipping through the appropriate interpretations. This, too, is frequently made more difficult because the actual behaviors that the professional in the group had been showing may have played right into the prejudices and hostilities generated by the professional status.

Participating in a group consisting solely of other group therapists prevents this particular dynamic. It is certainly a viable choice and one long encouraged by the American Group Psychotherapy Association (AGPA) at its annual institutes. Likewise, there are many group therapy possibilities set up "for therapists only" by the affiliate societies of AGPA and by institutions around the country.

Therapy or Process Group

The literature on the training of group therapists is replete with debates on whether the experiential part of training should be a true psychotherapy group or a "process" group. This same question must be faced by the therapist seeking a group experience. Some authors (Sadock & Kaplan, 1971; Woody, 1971) insist that only a therapy group can provide all the benefits of a therapeutic experience, but others believe that any group that studies its own processes is beneficial (Garwood, 1967; Lakin, Lieberman, & Whitaker, 1969). AGPA, in its model training regulations (1978), makes the distinction between the two types of groups and declares a clear preference in favor of the therapy group for the training of group psychotherapists.

The fact that both types of groups are mentioned in AGPA guidelines does not mean that there is much clarity about the differences between the two. The list of distinguishing features described in Table 1 is meant as an aid in clarifying the demarcation. I realize that some of my colleagues will disagree and that most of the differences are matters only of degree and not of substance. Some process groups are, in fact, quite individual-focused, and some therapy groups are almost entirely group-focused. Nevertheless, the differences described in Table 1 are useful as theoretical points of departure. They can also be used in formulating a contract between a leader and prospective group members.

Whichever form of group experience one chooses, there still appears to be an ethical imperative to be clear about the chosen format. It causes great resentment and fear if one promises participants a group-process study group and then turns it into a traditional psychotherapy group. Although either version is likely to be beneficial to its members, the group that has a clear contract from the outset about its goals and its parameters will ultimately be more successful.

Closed- or Open-Ended?

If learning about group dynamics is one of the more prominent goals in choosing a therapeutic experience, it is desirable to work with closed-ended groups. They offer the participants a better view of the developmental stages within the life of the group. The formation and changes of norms and roles over time can be ob-

TABLE 1. Distinguishing features of the two types of groups for therapists

Group Aspect	Group Therapy	Group Process Experience
Goal	Amelioration of personal pathology	Affective and cognitive learning about group dynamics
Intervention focus	More individual	More group-as-a-whole
Composition	Therapists only or together with nontherapists	All therapists (or trainees)
Self-concept of members	Patients	Students, participants
Cognitive component (lectures, readings, etc.)	Absent	Present

served better if the timeframe of the group has been set from the beginning. However, being in a closed-ended group may not be very realistic in light of the fact that most therapists conduct open-ended groups in private practice and clinic and hospital settings. The disruption of the natural flow of group dynamics caused by periodic terminations of old members and assimilations of new ones is part of the process with which the leader has to cope. Participating in such a group provides the members with an experience closest to that of the patients dealt with in their own work.

Intervention Foci

Borriello (1979) describes three types of interventions a group therapist can choose to make while working with a group. An interpretation can be focused on: the group as a whole, the interpersonal interaction between two members, or the personality and personal problems of one member. Depending on the focus chosen most often, the group will take on a specific quality. Although most group therapists use a combination of approaches, some are so group-focused that they will never make a person-centered interpretation, whereas others are person-centered to the point where the therapy is essentially an individual therapy conducted in the presence of others.

Whichever focus one chooses, it appears important to make these choices knowingly and with some forethought rather than merely to "roll with the punches" and come up with whatever interpretation seems to be called for at the moment. The preferred focus of the leader determines the type of group experience the participants will ultimately have. Thus, for the group therapist seeking an experience for himself or herself, it is worth knowing the intervention preference of the potential leader.

There is no overall rule as to which intervention focus is best for a group of psychotherapists. The group-as-a-whole approach tends to provide a greater amount of learning of group dynamics and generally reduces resistance among the participants to a more bearable level. However, just as a psychotherapy group can be legitimate and effective if conducted at a personal intervention level, the same can be true for a group for professionals.

Structured Exercises

The understanding of group dynamics can often be enhanced considerably by structured exercises as proposed by Pfeiffer and Jones (1971). Used at the right moment, the group can learn a great deal about its own issues and its own internal structure through a sociogram or communication exercise. However, such exercises require some risk-taking behavior on the part of the leader. There is always a chance that an exercise will backfire, that it will demonstrate something totally different from what one had planned, that it will disturb the group and increase resistance, or that it will become a source of embarrassment. Despite these risks, exercises are valuable and provide a considerable increase in learning. Interminable intellectual discussions can effectively be cut short by a drastic visible demonstration of a major group issue. The sociometric pattern on the wall may be the picture worth a thousand words.

Instrumentation

Using research instruments during the course of a therapy group can have an effect similar to that of a structured exercise. Dies (1980) offered a sampling of available instruments that can be used for this purpose. It includes tools like the Hill Interaction Matrix-B (Hill, 1977), the Group Atmosphere Scale (Silbergeld et al., 1975), and the Interaction Process Analysis (Bales, 1950). There are two additions to his list that I have used with some success in groups that I have led:

1. The Group Climate Questionnaire, Short Form (GCQ-S), by K. R. MacKenzie (1981). This instrument has shown itself to be an excellent, quick indicator of the mood and atmosphere in a group. It is sensitive to changes in group climate, which can then be reported back to the group, stimulating more discussion of its own developmental stage and possible resistances.
2. The DEST Test, by J. Durkin (1981). This instrument is closely tied in with the theory of group development and group roles proposed by Beck (1981). It focuses on roles taken by people in a group. It gives members an opportunity to see how their perceptions of themselves fit with the group's perception of them. It also permits insights into overrepresentation or underrepresentation of certain prototypal roles within a group.

The introduction of research instruments not only enhances the group's understanding of its progress and current issues. It also imparts a certain attitude towards research. Group therapy and practice are then no longer seen as antithetical to each other—as some therapists seem to think—but are presented as complementary: good group research enhances the practice of group therapy by making it more effective; the practice of group psychotherapy conversely helps to specify questions worth asking and worth answering through research.

Further, introducing research instruments can teach the group that research is easy to conduct and can move a group forward in great strides. It can thus, by acquainting group therapists with available group research methods, bridge the gap between practice and research (Coché & Dies, 1981).

A Forum for Supervision

Some leaders of groups for therapists encourage their members to discuss problems they are encountering in the groups they are leading. Although this is a legitimate use of group time, one should decide in advance if one wants to run a group with this as part of the agenda. There is certainly a danger that such discussions lead to much intellectualization and an elegant effort on everybody's part to stay away from the dynamics of one's own group by describing those of another one. The choice needs to be made on the basis of the needs of the members, their other resources for supervision, and the constraints of the institutional setting.

Intermittent Restructuring

The groups that my coworkers and I have led underwent constant changes in the format used. Human beings can be amazingly creative in the ways in which they resist a task once they feel unsafe. Because our groups for therapists took place in an institutional setting and consisted of people who were also working with one another, concerns about confidentiality and hierarchical issues were natural and at times caused much anxiety. We therefore had to reshape our style of working, the requirements and the constraints we placed on the group, and the way in which we combined cognitive and experiential learning in a process of continual readjustment. At times, we could trust that the group's own process and the need of the members to learn would take care of excessive resistances. At other times, however, a purposeful and even forceful intervention from the group leaders was necessary. Without such intervention, the group was occasionally in danger of becoming stale or nonproductive. Frequently, absences, latenesses, or outright complaints were indicators that something needed to be done to get things back on the right track.

COMMON GROUP THERAPEUTIC ISSUES

Groups for therapists present problems that are not genuinely different from problems found in any group. However, they can take on a special quality or be exacerbated by the fact that the members are group therapists.

Subgroupings

In any therapy group there will be times when one faction forms a coalition against another. Such coalitions can be on the basis of gender, race, or other demographic features, but more frequently, they are based on disagreements over the direction the group "should" take. In groups of therapists, the fact that the members may come from different mental health disciplines or different buildings within the institution can lead to the formation of coalitions, which in turn may insist on specific directions toward which they want to push the group. The group leader may have certain allegiances, too, and will at times collude with one of the factions or at least be identified as one of "them." A multidisciplinary co-leader team is a great protection against this pitfall. Otherwise, the interventions and interpretations that must be made to move the group out of its factional disputes need to be made more often, more skillfully, and perhaps more forcefully.

Dependency

Dependency is one of the stages described by Bennis and Shepard (1956) in which a group can remain stuck while avoiding work. Although this phase is quite natural, particularly for beginning groups, it can become more poignant and more difficult to overcome in a therapy group for clinicians. Having so much at stake in terms of their professional status and their acceptance within the group, members are understandably frightened and therefore likely to lean on the leaders not merely for direction for the group but also for precepts and guidance for their own within-the-group behavior and the setting of group norms. Here the leader has a fertile field for meaningful and well-placed interpretations that can move the group forward, heighten self-awareness, and provide growth experiences for the members to enable them to take more responsibility for the life of their group and for their own lives as well.

Scapegoating

Beck (1981) describes scapegoating in detail. This role, like all others, develops in the interchange between the role-bearer and the group. He considers the scapegoat to be one of the prime moving figures within the group, not only an object of dislike and derision, but also the representative of a disliked out-group. This phenomenon can frequently be observed in groups of therapists, too. If one of the departments within an institution is represented by only one person in the group, and all the others have more than one representative, it is possible for that person to be chosen as the first target. Scapegoats tend to contribute to this process by frequently showing behaviors that irritate other group members even though they may actually be very much in the interest of group progress. Occasionally the leader may have to intervene in order to prevent the actual ejection of such a member. Most often, however, a few specific group-as-a-whole interpretations can help the group get out of its attack mode. At times, one other group member will become tired of excessive focusing on the scapegoat and shift to a more fruitful direction.

Between-Session Activities

Interaction among group members between sessions has been the subject of some debate in the group psychotherapy literature (Yalom, 1975; Kaplan & Sadock, 1983). Although these authors warn against such contacts and suggest that groups have rules prohibiting them, many therapists feel that anything goes as long as it is discussible. In an institution where people have to work with each other and also interact in such places as cafeterias and snack bars, a prohibition against between-session contact would be ludicrous. However, some such contacts can cause severe problems for the group. Members may get together to work out differences between them that arose in a group session and thus deprive the group of an important dynamic. Worse than that, they may get together in order to discuss the pathology of a member who is not party to this discussion. When such behavior becomes group knowledge, it is likely to greatly upset the other members and to lead to the formulation of a group norm prohibiting extra-group contact, which may be impossible to enforce. The leader of such a group experience is well advised to be clear about his or her own preference in this matter and the rationale for a decision. I am most comfortable with allowing members to interact between sessions with the proviso that they discuss their interactions in the group and stay away from extensive discussions of absent members.

Also, I prefer to work with groups that clearly articulate their norms.

Acting Out

The above mentioned between-session activities, and occasional lapses in confidentiality or sexual activities between members, are the most common forms of serious acting out, yet they are rather rare in groups of clinicians. More commonly, acting out will take the more subtle forms of innuendo, sarcasm, or excessive silences. When these occur, they are signs that something is wrong in the group and has not been dealt with directly. At that point some attention to the developmental phase of the group is indicated. Group-as-a-whole interventions that focus on the developmental issue rather than the form of the acting out are most likely to be effective in moving the group forward and in squelching the undesired behavior.

An event that occurred in a group of professionals I co-led a few years ago may serve as an example. The group was quite clearly stuck in a developmental phase called "disenchantment" (Bennis & Shepard, 1956). It seemed unable to move on to the next phase, which would have entailed more interdependence and intimacy between the members. At that point, two women in the group spent an evening at the home of one of them, discussing the group and its problems at length, thereby violating a norm this group had set. When they confessed their behavior in the next session, they were at first chastised for their "acting out." The group then, however, with little help from their leaders, began to see that these women had achieved the degree of intimacy and mutual trust the group was longing for. Observing this was the impetus the group needed to stop stalling and to move on to the next stage.

In groups of professionals the danger of acting out is rivaled by the pernicious habit of some members of labeling too many behaviors as "acting out" or "inappropriate." I have learned to watch these words as indicators that a group may be engaged in very rigid norm setting and enforcing. Frequently it is not the whole group but only one particular member who is creating a powerful position for himself or herself by becoming the legislator and guardian of the group norms.

To make matters worse, the behaviors marked as "acting out"

are often either innocuous or actually desirable: for example, self-disclosures or expressions of affect. Labeling them as "inappropriate" causes considerable fear and inhibition, leading to interminable silences, bland intellectualizations, and other symptoms of a group in trouble. The leader of a group of therapists, therefore, needs to be particularly watchful in the normative phase of a group.

GROUP THERAPY FOR THE
NOVICE GROUP THERAPIST

This chapter has dealt mostly with the issues involved in the conduct of group therapy for the experienced practitioner. The following section sheds some light on problems encountered in groups for therapy trainees.

The training of group therapists has been a subject of great interest in the group therapy literature. In 1980, Dies found 200 published articles on this topic, plus several reviews. Although a plethora of different teaching modes has been proposed so far, most authors and reviewers (Coché, 1977; and Dies, 1980, for examples) recommend some type of group experience as the crucial ingredient of a comprehensive training program. Group psychotherapy for the aspiring therapist has been advocated by many (M. Berger, 1969; Sadock & Kaplan, 1971; Berman, 1975; Shapiro, 1978). As early as 1947, Samuel Hadden, a past president of AGPA, proposed group therapy sessions as a way of introducing novices to therapy. The response from his (medical) students was enthusiastic. They considered this step as revolutionary, "like coming off the benches and standing next to the surgeon during the operation" (Hadden, 1982).

The endorsement of group therapy for future group therapists has grown continually since then and is now part of the model training program proposed by AGPA (1978), which lists as one of the desired requirements "Participation as a patient in group psychotherapy for a minimum of 120 hours of which a maximum of 30 hours in a group process experience may be substituted."

However, endorsement of participation in therapy groups for beginning group leaders has never been unanimous and still is not. M. Berger's (1969) article extolling the advantages of groups for group therapists was quickly followed by an article by I. Berger (1969) pointing out many of the difficulties and problems involved in such an undertaking. Shapiro (1978) voices similar concerns, many of which are addressed in this chapter.

Similarities to Groups for Advanced Therapists

Most of the issues described in the preceding pages also pertain to group trainees. Resistance is likely to be just as high as or even higher than in the advanced groups, institutional embeddedness is a major problem, and the first few sessions are likely to focus on the confidentiality problem. Furthermore, groups of novices are even more prone to develop extreme degrees of dependency and to use extraneous material as a means of avoiding within-group concerns.

Intermittent restructuring of the group format is even more necessary in groups for trainees. The resistances can take so many forms that creativity has to be one of the leader's prime attributes lest the group stagnate and the members stop learning and growing.

Grades and Evaluations

One aspect that sets trainees' groups apart from groups in which accomplished practitioners get together is that in a training program it may be expected that the group leaders will grade the students on their degree or manner of participation in the group. This may be a requirement of the residency or doctoral program.

Concurring with Berman's (1975) and Shapiro's (1978) warnings, I have always eschewed this practice. In the process groups I have led, I have insisted that no grades be required on the members' degree or type of participation. Resistance is enough of a problem; the threat of an ultimate evaluation based on how one "performs" in group would in all likelihood destroy the affective as well as cognitive learning. And to demand self-disclosure from participants under the threat of a negative evaluation is ethically questionable.

Sometimes, even though the leaders may not write a formal evaluation, their membership on the faculty of the residency or doctoral program can still arouse much concern among the group participants. A workable solution to this problem may be the hiring of a group leader who is not a member of the institutional faculty (Berman, 1975; Shapiro, 1978).

Student Role

Many novices in group therapy are already advanced members of their mental health profession and therefore reluctant to assume the role of a student again. Directly or in more subtle ways, they demand to be treated with special consideration for their status, or they are lax in their handling of such homework assignments as reading or keeping logs. This in turn can cause considerable resentment from lower-ranking members of the group and can add to the tension in the room.

In one of our groups the presence of a high-ranking member of the institutional hierarchy created precisely this problem. Though outwardly denying that she wanted any kind of special consideration, she was so tardy in completing assignments that her actions belied her words. When she began to miss sessions because important committee meetings "made it impossible to attend the group" it was pointed out to her that she was in fact choosing the institutional committee over the group. This, together with a discussion of the role-conflicts involved, changed her manner of participation considerably and relieved much of the tension and anger felt by the junior participants.

Integration of Cognitive and Experiential Learning

Ever since the trailblazing article by M. Berger (1969), there have been numerous proposals on how to combine the didactic and experiential aspects of the learning to be imparted to future group therapists (Dies, 1980; Gazda, 1975; Bascue, 1978). In our groups at Friends Hospital, we tried a variety of approaches. At one time, we alternated between cognitive and process sessions. Another time, we set an a priori schedule of six theoretical sessions to be followed by six process sessions, alternating for 42 sessions. In more recent years we used a format in which the group would run for 75 minutes, after which 15 minutes were spent on discussing what went on in the session itself. This was combined with a list of suggested readings.

Another method tried was assigning homework, specifically the writing of a one- or two-page log about each session. This would then be read later by the leader and provide information on members' perceptions of their group. From this the leader could derive hints on trouble spots in the group or about theoretical topics worth pursuing. The disadvantage was that if a problem emerged in a group, the writing, reading, and returning of the log would entail a two-week lag, often causing complicated communication difficulties.

Whatever format we used, the group was always able to abuse it for resistance purposes, a danger already pointed out by I. Berger (1969). Sometimes groups would spend all their time in meaningful and self-disclosing interactions at the expense of their cognitive learning. They would do so purposefully, in order to avoid more intellectual tasks including studying the assigned readings. Other groups would spend their time in esoteric, theoretical discussions, obviously to avoid having to deal with some difficult interpersonal problems within the group. Whenever such excesses were observed, the leaders usually needed to intervene, but were frequently assisted by those members of the group who themselves had become uncomfortable with the imbalance.

Learning Leadership Behaviors

One of the greatest advantages of a therapy group for trainees is that the fledgling therapists learn a large variety of leadership behaviors merely by watching the modeling of their leader. Beginning therapists rarely choose their preferred mode of psychotherapy by making conscious choices between analytic, rational-emotive, or other therapeutic modalities on the basis of their readings. More often these choices are the result of emulating an inspiring preceptor.

In the life of a group the leader has to deal with many situations not discussed in textbooks. Observing a therapist at work provides the student with an armamentarium of available responses when situations occur in their own groups. For example, I have had long discussions with graduate students in clinical psychology about the advisability of self-disclosure of personal data by a group leader to his or her group. In observing the students at work, I found that their actual self-disclosing behavior was determined much more by the style of their model therapist, who frequently was the leader of their process group, than by weighty debates they had heard or been involved in.

Discovery of Personal Problems

It is possible that in the course of a process group the leader will discover serious personal problems in one member. These can be so severe that one has to question whether this person is fit to be a therapist. Because the group is part of a training program, the emotional impairment of a trainee cannot be taken lightly. The fact that most of these groups work under a contract of confidentiality prevents the therapist from handling the problem directly with the training director and this creates a complicated ethical dilemma. However, there are a few possible solutions. First, it is likely that the trainee is also being observed by a number of other supervisors and trainers. If the disturbance is serious enough, it is likely to be visible to these people, who are not bound by a confidentiality rule. Secondly, the group leader frequently has a special relationship of trust and respect with the trainee and can make a recommendation for personal therapy in such a way that the trainee will follow up on it instead of becoming defensive and indignant. Thirdly, if participation in the group is truly voluntary, most trainees who already have doubts regarding their emotional stability usually will prefer not to participate in such a group. Thus, their pathology will most likely become evident in the process of being supervised for their therapeutic work rather than in the group.

Prior Experience

Since the 1970s, when growth groups were proliferating, many training programs in psychology and social work have been including process groups in their curricula. Thus, many individuals joining a therapists' group have had some prior experience in a process group. That is frequently more of a burden than a help, because members carry their preconceived notions as to "what a group should be about" into the new group and try to foist the norms and expectations from prior groups onto the present group. This in turn causes stiff resistance from those who have had different or anxiety-arousing past experiences. The other members who have had no prior experience at all tend to find the sudden injunction to "let it all hang out" rather frightening.

Voluntariness

The fact that the group members are also members of a training program sometimes means that they have only limited choice over whether to attend. Depending on the particular program, there may be either a direct injunction that participation in the group is a prerequisite to graduating from the program; or participation is said to be voluntary, but there is a clear understanding that non-participation will be frowned upon by those in power. Finally, there are programs in which the participation is truly voluntary and where trainees who choose not to join the group can still enjoy all the rights and privileges of their training program without any reprisals. It has been our experience that this kind of freedom not only allows potentially shaky members to stay out of the group but also sets a very positive tone for the group, in that everybody knows that all are involved because they want to be there, and they can truly invest their energy in making the most of it.

SOME FINAL CONSIDERATIONS

In recent years, group psychotherapy research has shown with increasing clarity that group therapists not only can do much for the amelioration of human suffering but also can do harm, especially if they are using their groups for the pursuit of personal gain (Hartley, Roback, & Abramovitz, 1979). An experiential group for therapists can help teachers and leaders to detect potentially harmful persons. It can occasionally help the student to change in a desirable direction or it can stimulate his or her supervisors to redirect the career path of the potentially harmful therapist into a more innocuous, nontherapeutic direction, thus saving some future patients from possible iatrogenic disturbances.

An experiential group for therapists can also impart ethical standards through teaching and modeling (Gazda, 1975). This is yet another argument for conducting such groups.

Although it is my conviction that self-study groups for therapy trainees are desirable and truly help in making novice group therapists more effective and more responsible in the work they do, there is unfortunately no research to prove this point. There are some—albeit conflicting—data available on the effects of personal therapy for individual therapists (Strupp, 1955; Holt & Luborsky, 1958; Peebles, 1980; other chapters in this book), but no such information appears currently available on the effects of group therapy for group therapists. We have reached a stage now in which a generation of new group therapists has been trained in programs that included an experiential component, and we still do not know with any reasonable degree of reliability whether this experiential part is as valuable as we have come to believe. It is hoped that researchers will find the courage and the funding to investigate whether group therapists who had an experiential component in their training are indeed better equipped than group therapists who did not. Until then, we have to assume the superiority of such training on faith, random observation, and personal experience.

References

American Group Psychotherapy Association. Guidelines for the training of group psychotherapists. New York: AGPA, 1978.

Bales, R. F. *Interaction process analysis: A method for the study of small groups.* Reading, Mass.: Addison-Wesley, 1950.

Bascue, L. D. A conceptual model for training group therapists. *International Journal of Group Psychotherapy.* 1978, *28*, 445–452.

Beck, A. P. Developmental characteristics of the system-forming process. In J. E. Durkin, *Living Groups.* New York: Brunner/Mazel, 1981.

Beck, A. P., & Peters, L. The research evidence for distributed leadership in therapy groups. *The International Journal of Group Psychotherapy,* 1981, *31*, 43–71.

Bennis, W. G., & Shepard, H. A. A theory of group development. *Human Relations,* 1956, *9*, 415–437.

Berger, I. L. Resistances to the learning process in group dynamics programs. *American Journal of Psychiatry,* 1969, *126*, 850–857.

Berger, M. M. Experiential and didactic aspects of training in therapeutic group approaches. *American Journal of Psychiatry,* 1969, *126*, 845–850.

Berman, A. L. Group psychotherapy training. *Small Group Behavior,* 1975, *6*, 325–344.

Borriello, J. F. Intervention foci in group psychotherapy. In L. R. Wolberg and M. L. Aronson (Eds.), *Group Psychotherapy 1979.* New York: Stratton Intercontinental, 1979.

Coché, E., Training of Group Therapists. In F. W. Kaslow and Associates. *Supervision, consultation, and staff training in the helping professions.* San Francisco: Jossey-Bass, 1977.

Coché, E., & Dies, R. R. Integrating research findings into the practice of group therapy. *Psychotherapy: Theory, research and practice.* 1981, *18*, 410–415.

Coché, E., Dies, R. R., and Albrecht, E. Results of the 1982 Annual Institutes of the American Group Psychotherapy Association. Unpublished data, presented at the Annual Meeting of the AGPA, February 15, 1982.

Dies, R. R. Group psychotherapy: training and supervision. In A. K. Hess (Ed.), *Psychotherapy Supervision.* New York: Wiley, 1980.

Dies, R. R. Personal communication, March, 1983.

Durkin, J. The DEST Test, (1981). Available from Dr. Durkin at B 4 Heritage Village, R. D. No. 2, Landenberg, Pa 19350.

Garwood, D. S. The significance and dynamics of sensitivity training programs. *International Journal of Group Psychotherapy,* 1967, *17*, 457–472.

Gazda, G. M. (Ed.) *Basic approaches to group psychotherapy and group counseling* (2nd ed.). Springfield, Ill.: Thomas, 1975.

Hadden, Samuel. Personal communication, November 15, 1982.

Hartley, D., Roback, H. B., & Abramovitz, S. I. Deterioration effects in encounter groups. In H. B. Roback, S. I. Abramovitz, and D. S. Strassberg (Eds.), *Group psychotherapy research: Commentaries and selected readings*. Huntington, N.Y.: Krieger, 1979.

Hill, W. F. Hill Interaction Matrix (HIM): The conceptual framework, derived rating scales, and an updated bibliography. *Small Group Behavior*, 1977, *8*, 251–258.

Holt, R. and Luborsky, L. *Personality patterns of psychiatrists*. New York: Basic Books, 1958.

Kaplan, H. I, & Sadock, B. J. Structured interactional group psychotherapy. In: H. I. Kaplan and B. J. Sadock (Eds.) *Comprehensive Group Psychotherapy* (2nd ed.). Baltimore: Williams & Wilkins, 1983.

Lakin, M., Lieberman, M. A., & Whitaker, D. S. Issues in the training of group psychotherapists. *International Journal of Group Psychotherapy*, 1969, *19*, 307–325.

MacKenzie, K. R. Measurement of group climate. *International Journal of Group Psychotherapy*, 1981, *31*, 287–295.

MacKenzie, K. R. The group climate questionnaire, 1981. Obtainable from Dr. MacKenzie, Health Sciences Center, Faculty of Medicine, University of Calgary, Calgary, Alberta, Canada.

Peebles, M. J. Personal therapy and ability to display empathy, warmth and genuineness in psychotherapy. *Psychotherapy: Theory, Research and Practice*, 1980, *17*, 258–262.

Pfeiffer, J. W., & Jones, J. E. *A handbook of structured experiences for human relations training*. Volumes I–III. Iowa City: University Associates, 1971.

Sadock, B. J., & Kaplan, H. I. Training and standards in group psychotherapy. In H. I. Kaplan and B. J. Sadock, *Comprehensive Group Psychotherapy*. Baltimore: Williams & Wilkins, 1971.

Shapiro, J. E. *Methods of group psychotherapy and encounter*. Itasca, Ill.: Peacock, 1978.

Silbergeld, S., Koenig, G. R., Manderscheid, R. H., Meeker, B. F., & Horning, C. A. Assessment of environment-therapy systems: The group atmosphere scale. *Journal of Consulting and Clinical Psychology*, 1975, *43*, 460–469.

Strupp, H. H. The effect of the psychotherapist's personal analysis upon his techniques. *Journal of Consulting Psychology*, 1955, *19*, 197–204.

Thelen, H. *Dynamics of groups at work*. Chicago: University of Chicago Press, 1954.

Woody, R. H. Self-understanding seminars: The effects of group psychotherapy in counselor training. *Counselor Education and Supervision*. 1971, *10*, 112–119.

Yalom, I. D. *The theory and practice of group psychotherapy* (2nd ed.). New York: Basic Books, 1975.

Notes

1. Most of the experiences that form the basis of this chapter were gathered while I was on the staff of Friends Hospital in Philadelphia.

2. I would like to thank Steven Cohen, PH.D., and B. A. Lief, M.D., for the thoughts and ideas they provided during their years of working with me as coleaders in groups for therapists. I also want to thank Jay Efran, PH.D., Richard Peters, PH.D., and Marta Vago, M.S.W., for the many insights they provided while leading groups for therapists in which I was privileged to participate.

EDITOR'S COMMENTARY

When the Group is the Medium

In this chapter, Erich Coché discusses group therapy for group therapist trainees and advanced practitioners. He looks at the difference between process groups and didactic groups, indicating that whichever modality is the preference, it should be clearly stated in the contract with the group. Throughout, he argues persuasively for maximum clarity in the working out of objectives and rules governing group behavior. Given that therapy groups are often made up of people who work together within the same institution, he suggests that issues surrounding confidentiality and feelings about someone's status in the institution hierarchy are quite marked. These, plus institutional embeddedness, need to be discussed openly so that everyone can achieve some degree of comfort with them. It stands to reason that concerns about authority, confidentiality, and loss of privacy would be more marked within the institutional context, because group members are likely to know each other professionally and be concerned about their reputations if they engage in too much personal disclosure. He does not deal with groups of therapists who come together who do not work in the same setting—there might be some important differences such as less concern for what is happening in the institution.

He highlights the importance of people having a choice whether or not to belong. Where participation is mandatory, it is likely to have an impact on increasing the level of resistance. Another concern he raises, and justly, is that of trainees in a program who are required to have a group experience and be given a grade for this. This is an issue with which I struggled for many years when I taught a group therapy course in a graduate school psychology program. If one is teaching group therapy didactically, using the groups the students are leading as the content for analysis of process, the students are likely to press for a group experience with one another. Conversely, if one shifts into leading a group-therapy group, some students are likely to assert that they were not told in the catalogue that this would be part of the experience, and they resent it. Universities must make clear before the student comes into the program whether the group therapy will be taught as a process group experience or as a content-oriented course.

In training programs we do not suggest that students should
learn individual therapy by being in individual therapy with the in-
structor. They learn content of the therapy process, bring in a case
they are doing for classroom discussion and critique, or take it to a
supervisor. Perhaps the same principles should apply to the learning of group therapy.

There are numerous ethical questions raised. For any institution to make participation in a therapy experience mandatory is almost a contradiction in terms. To participate in group therapy can
be both a personal responsibility and a privilege. What are the responsibilities of the group leader if he or she realizes that a member of the group is severely disturbed? If the person is a trainee, is
there an obligation to report this to the teaching institution? If the
person is a member of an agency staff, what responsibility does the
leader carry for accountability to the agency—especially if he or
she, too, is a member of the staff? Coché indicates that the dysfunctional patterns will probably be picked up by another member
of the faculty who does not have a relationship that entails privileged communication with a member of the group. I think the issue is more complex than that. A therapist has a responsibility not
only to a group member but also to the patients, current and future, this person is likely to serve. Therefore, the therapist must at
least seriously consider recommending to this person that he or
she seek intensive individual therapy and suggest that perhaps at
this time being a therapist might be counterindicated.

As Coché indicates, we need a great deal more research on the
efficacy of therapy groups as a training technique for learning
group therapy. Also, the entire field could use some research base-
line for determining the effects on trainees of telling them that they
should be in individual therapy and that perhaps they should put
their work as a therapist temporarily on hold until they get some of
their own dilemmas straightened out. The legal ramifications are
manifold and need serious consideration.

Group therapy is certainly a medium that provides a sense of
belonging, a multidimensional reflection of how others see the
self, and a chance to do some critical self-searching within the context of a group experience. Confidentiality and institutional hierarchy issues as Coché casts them are in many ways related to the
boundary issues raised by other authors in this book.

8

Psychotherapy with Women Therapists

Judith Coché, PH.D.

There is an unmistakable phenomenon occurring around gender and psychotherapy, which involves all mental health professionals directly and all of their clients indirectly. A few examples:

1. Within the last month, the office phone at 2037 Delancey Place has rung at least six times—calls from different female psychotherapists living within a sixty-mile radius of center city Philadelphia—and the calls all start: "Hello, my name is _____ and you were suggested to me by _____, who said you do psychotherapy with therapists. I've worked in therapy before, but I am especially interested in working with a woman . . ."
2. My husband and I, partners in a joint practice, interviewed a male applicant for a research position who knew us only by reputation. He turned to me and said, "I understand that most of your work is with professional women." This statement is untrue since I work very frequently with families, couples, groups, and adolescents. However, what had been reported to him was my work with professional women.
3. A large percentage of my psychotherapy practice is with male clients: professional men, businessmen, fathers. In eight years I have received only two requests from a male psychotherapist for his own psychotherapy.

What is this phenomenon? Female psychotherapists are seeking other female psychotherapists to assist them in structuring their own, personal change. Moreover, the phenomenon is fairly recent: ten years ago, there were very few female psychotherapists in private practice in the Delaware Valley. Today there is a rapidly increasing core group with solid referral bases and waiting lists.

This chapter considers the issues involved in being a therapist for female psychotherapists. First, literature on psychotherapy with women and the lack of literature on psychotherapy with women therapists is briefly considered. Second, because of the paucity of published literature on the topic, the chapter reports on the results of asking female clients to help pinpoint the similarities and differences between doing psychotherapy with women therapists as compared with doing psychotherapy with other professional women. A questionnaire was distributed, which is discussed. Finally, after looking at the questionnaire data, some clinical, ethical, and developmental issues in working with female therapists and with other professional women are presented.

PSYCHOTHERAPY WITH WOMEN

One consequence of females' recognition of their equality with men in the Western world in the 1960s and 1970s is that educators and mental health professionals have come to understand that issues relating to women deserve their own emphasis. Courses on women's issues have become standard in most universities, and books and journal articles have begun to appear that are devoted exclusively to women in the psychotherapy process. Compendiums by Brodsky and Hare-Mustin (1980) and by Franks and Burtle (1974), and special issues of *The Counseling Psychologist* (Volume 8, 1979; Volume 6, 1976) and *Professional Psychology* (Volume 1, 1981) academically address the issue. Within the popular press, Maggie Scarf's *Unfinished Business* (1980) has received recent acclaim on the topic of psychotherapy with depressed women.

Moreover, research about psychotherapy process and outcome now includes data sections on the relationship between gender and psychotherapy. For example, Garfield and Bergin (1978) included sections on women in the chapters "Research on Therapist Variables in Relation to Process and Outcome" and "Research on Client Variables in Psychotherapy." Likewise, Gurman and Razin (1977) included material on client gender.

Main Recurrent Themes

Three themes running through writings on psychotherapy with women may be highlighted. One revolves around biology and destiny and considers the effect of genetic and hormonal differences on such life development issues as career performance and personality makeup. A second theme is role conflict as a major struggle for most females. Here the literature is concerned with the healthful development of roles for women as well as with what to do about role conflict within the psychotherapy setting. The third theme is the question of whether women function as disadvantaged members of the work force. Those authors who believe that they do, and most feminists would fall within this grouping, discuss how to ameliorate a situation that has been historically destructive to women.

Two themes in the literature are related to training issues for psychotherapists working with women: 1) whether psychotherapy is different with women clients than it is with men, and 2) whether classic psychoanalytically oriented individual therapy is theoretically and practically harmful to the women who participate in it.

Any female psychotherapist-in-training who wants to work with women needs to familiarize herself with the literature on psychotherapy with women, most of which has appeared within the last ten years. Social scientists (Brodsky and Hare-Mustin, 1980; Bardwick, 1971) who attest to the need for a comprehensive developmental study of the female socialization process as it is similar to and different from that of the male, deserve acknowledgement. There have been recent well-documented research efforts in understanding the socialization process in males, notably those by Gould (1978), Vaillant (1977), and Levinson (1978). However, these reporters agree that it is impossible to generalize to female life cycle issues from their studies. As Gilligan and Norman (1978) discuss, even Erikson's developmental schema is based primarily on male psychological development, against which female psychological development must be seen as deviant. For example, Stewart (1977) describes that the dreams that women form tend to have a strong relational component, whereas the dreams of men in Levinson's sample were more individualistic.

Gilligan and Norman (1978) state that for men, identity precedes intimacy and generativity in the optimal cycle of development, but that for women these tasks seemed fused. Intimacy can precede or proceed simultaneously with identity because feminine identity develops as it is known through relationship with others.

It is well established that certain differences exist between the sexes in childhood: girl children have greater verbal ability than boys, boys excel in visual-spatial ability; boys excel in mathematical ability; boys are more aggressive (Maccoby and Jacklin, 1974, pp. 351–52). If the goal of the psychotherapeutic process is to maximize life satisfaction and functioning, a thorough knowledge of child and adult development is fundamental to the skills of psychotherapists. However, until more extensive theoretical, clinical, and research data are collected on the way females develop, psychotherapists will continue to find themselves practicing a science with insufficient observational and theoretical foundations. A major longitudinal study of female development, of the type conducted by Cox (1970) for young adults or Levinson (1978) for adult males, is long overdue, despite the recent surge of written attention to women's issues in the social sciences.

PSYCHOTHERAPY WITH PSYCHOTHERAPISTS

Many female psychotherapists have had personal experience in therapy, but virtually nothing about this has become part of the literature on psychotherapy. A review of *Psychological Abstracts* and of major edited works within the last ten years brought to light only one piece of research having to do with women therapists as psychotherapy consumers. Welnar et al. (1979) compared psychiatric disorders among physicians and PH.D. professional women. They found a higher percentage of psychopathology, notably depression, among physicians than among PH.D.s and found the highest percentage of psychopathology among psychiatrists. This finding would be very interesting if the data were more clearly presented and extensive. They interviewed only 214 women; this author estimated that 35 were psychiatrists. They caution that their findings are based on too small a sample to be considered meaningful and agree that more research in the area is necessary.

Let us turn briefly to the literature prior to this volume. Here, too, it is valuable to recognize three thematic threads. The first concerns whether psychotherapists should have personal psychotherapy and, if so, for what reason, with whom, and when in their training process. Sank and Prout (1978) state the frequently held belief that psychotherapy is worthwhile for the fledgling therapist and that the therapist's problem areas are best dealt with as a patient. Disadvantages they describe include the expense involved and the potential inadvisability of stirring up conflicts during the training period, when a therapist is already in conflict. Garfield (1977, p. 79) believes that "perhaps a majority of psychotherapists have themselves undergone some form of personal therapy." He suggests that psychotherapy is a good idea for therapists-in-training if it increases their effectiveness as psychotherapists, and he goes on to review a few studies that attempt to address the issue. Like Sank and Prout (1978), Garfield (1977, p. 80) states, "definitive data on the importance of personal therapy for the effective professional functioning of the psychotherapist is not available." He continues that most individuals who have undergone personal psychotherapy stress its value and reminds us that most postgraduate psychoanalytic institutes and most psychotherapy training programs require or endorse personal therapy. "Such requirements appear, however, to be based upon conviction and belief rather than on scientific evidence, a pattern quite familiar to the field of psychotherapy."

Hans Strupp (1955) has long been considered a leader in the area of outcome research in the psychotherapy process. His doctoral dissertation concerned the effect of the psychotherapist's "personal analysis" upon his techniques. Comparing 30 therapists who had undergone "personal analysis" with 11 other therapists who had not been analyzed, he concluded that "analyzed practitioners" tend to be more active, tend to prefer interpretations, silence, structuring responses in dealing with transference phenomena, and tend to be more exploratory in dealing with schizoid productions of seriously disturbed patients. He, too, however, warned that his sample was limited and his findings were best considered tentative.

A second theme concerns the personality, dynamics, and personal history of those individuals who choose the profession of psychotherapy. Racusin, Abramowitz, & Winter (1981) found that psychotherapists' family relationships were stressful and higher in physical illness, difficulties in expression of affect, and adolescent struggles over independence than those of other groups of professionals. A high degree of stress in the family of origin of psycho-

therapists was also found, and the conclusion was drawn retro-
spectively that many therapists had responded to these issues
when they were children, by trying to become nurturing within
their own families. This contradicts findings by Henry, Sims, &
Spray (1973) who reported that therapists' family relationships
were generally positive and that they experienced relatively little
emotional stress during childhood. It is obvious from these contra-
dictory findings that, as in the first theme, it is not possible to rely
on research to learn about stress in the earlier years of life of those
individuals who become psychotherapists.

Research offers only tentative and inconclusive information
about the benefits of personal psychotherapy in increasing the effectiveness of the therapist in doing psychotherapy. Therefore,
those clinical supervisors who espouse the value of a personal
therapy experience in increasing the effectiveness of a psychotherapy trainee need to be aware that they are operating on the basis of
personal assumption or clinical experience but not on the basis of
scientific evidence. This is not to deny the potential value of the
psychotherapy experience for the fledgling therapist; nowhere else
can one learn as well about the experience of being in therapy,
what it feels like to be a client, and how one's past has contributed
to professional choice of career and "thorny" problems as a therapist. However, it is humbling to consider that there is little or no
research documentation of the value of receiving therapy on doing
therapy.

The third and perhaps most powerful theme in writings on
psychotherapy for psychotherapists, is the need for role models by
the developing therapist as part of her personal and professional
training. The American Psychological Association formed a 1978
Task Force on Women, which addressed the importance of female
role models for the acculturation of women into nontraditional occupational roles. O'Connell (1978) addressed the isolation of
women professionals who not only felt that they were competing
against insurmountable odds, but also that they were competing
alone. O'Connell and Russo (1978) gathered a series of biographies
on eminent women in psychology. They quoted Goldstein (1979),
who stated that men in psychology take the presence of same-sex
role models and the concomitant facilitative effect for granted, but
that women cannot do this and often must exert heroic, and somewhat isolated, efforts to achieve their goal.

Clinical Observations

Two points from my clinical experience bear mention. Earlier in this chapter, I mentioned that numerous female, but only two male psychotherapists had requested therapy with me, although my practice contains many male clients who are not psychotherapists. This puzzling situation may be explained by Goldstein's statement of the importance of male role models for male psychotherapists: the impact of a therapist upon a client exerts powerful modeling dimensions in shaping the client's Weltanschauung, and it may be the search for someone to act as a role model that has led male therapists to other male therapists for treatment. For example, Malcolm (1982), in an interview with a male psychoanalyst concerning the modeling process as part of the training analysis, said that modeling after one's own therapist can go as far as learning how to dress.

My clinical experience with women in other professions indicates that the feeling of "competing against insurmountable odds" is not limited to female psychotherapists. In a workshop of which I was co-leader at the 1983 Fourth Annual Conference on Women in Health Care Medicine, members of the workshop, most notably female medical students, confided their overwhelming impression that they would have to be "superwomen" in order to combine careers with meaningful family relationships; they expressed their frustration at the difficulty of meeting men who wanted to be equal partners in a coprofessional couple relationship. The "double bind" they talked about has also been described by women therapists in their own psychotherapy: the more competent they become professionally, the harder it seems to be to find men whose egos do not need a "weaker" seeming woman who is available for intimacy at the male's convenience. Therefore, the difficult social situation can increase the sense of isolation described by O'Connell (1978) and can lead women professionals to feel caught in a bind between feeling loved and being professionally successful.

Abroms (1977) describes the supervision process as a metatherapy, noting the parallels between the two processes and the capacity for a supervisory trainee to learn about the process of psychotherapy through the supervisory relationship. Analyzing Abroms' concept another way, psychotherapy can also be thought of as a metasupervision for the therapist-in-training. Through the experience of psychotherapy as a psychotherapy consumer with a competent therapist on whom the fledgling therapist can model herself, the novice psychotherapist learns about various aspects and levels of the psychotherapy process. Learning can include everything from the superficialities of appearance and demeanor to the deepest levels of resistance, transference, and countertransference. This concept is of great interest in light of the following discussion about the responses to the questionnaires.

COMPARISON BETWEEN PSYCHOTHERAPISTS AND OTHER WOMEN PROFESSIONALS AS PSYCHOTHERAPY CONSUMERS

Methodology

As has been mentioned, women therapists and women in general have been seeking female therapists with increasing frequency. Maracek and Johnson (in Brodsky & Hare-Mustin, 1980) state that "better-educated individuals, younger individuals and women are more likely than their counterparts to prefer female therapists." I have eight years of experience as a psychotherapist with female therapists, and since there is so little documented information about this area, I developed a questionnaire consisting of five questions. Ten women therapists and ten women professionals with similar life profiles were asked to respond briefly. The questionnaires were mailed with a cover letter explaining that this author was writing a book chapter about women but not telling the respondee the exact subject matter. Within five days, 13 of the 20 questionnaires had been completed and returned, indicating that these women were willing to provide personal information to assist in increasing broader knowledge about adult female development. Only two women, both radical feminist therapists, refused to participate. Three nontherapists stated willingness, but neglected to complete the questionnaire. Data analysis is thus based on 8 therapist and 7 nontherapist responses, by professional females ages 28–38. The questions follow:

1. Name two issues in your own therapy that seemed central to your personal development during and after your psychotherapy.

2. Name two issues in your own therapy that seemed central to your professional development (within your own field) both during and after your psychotherapy.
3. In your work professionally with women, how do your female clients/patients/customers remind you of yourself? Which issues in their lives touch closest to your own issues? How do the similarities affect your capacity to work with these women?
4. Which qualities did you look for in seeking your own therapist?
5. In your personal and professional opinion, which psychotherapy issues do you see as particularly relevant to women?

Dividing the responses into therapist and nontherapist categories, it became possible to look at the responses of the therapists as a group to the questions and to compare them to the responses of the nontherapists. Next, themes of general importance to all women and themes particularly relevant to women therapists were extracted. This extrapolation was done both by this author and by a research assistant who had never met any of these women and knew only which were therapists and which were not.

Three categories of response developed: qualities looked for in a therapist, characteristics relevant to the therapy process and the process of personal change, and issues of particular relevance to women personally and in the work world.

Since the study was too informal to be considered scientific research, the findings are discussed in a reflective rather than scientific manner, touching on the themes that seem to be particularly relevant to the topic at hand.

Patterns in Psychotherapy with Women

Both groups mentioned the desire for a female therapist who was active and direct and participated forthrightly in the psychotherapy process, who had a good reputation in the community, and who was accepting and understanding of the client's situation. However, the nontherapists were more interested in the reputation and the psychotherapy style, while the therapists stated an interest in finding someone to act as a role model who had a well-integrated theoretical background and a clear conceptual framework. One therapist said that she was quite pleased to be going to a "therapist's therapist"; another said that she had looked widely to find someone of good reputation. Comparing the two groups, it seemed that a woman who was choosing therapy as a personal growth experience was less concerned with finding a model than was a therapist who was choosing psychotherapy as a personal growth experience and as a way of learning how to proceed with her career. And, as I discuss later, there was a striking similarity between what the female therapists were looking for in choosing their own therapist and what Levinson (1978) describes about the mentoring process for men.

When asked to name two issues central to their personal development in psychotherapy, respondents in both categories agreed overwhelmingly that lack of self-worth and feelings of inadequacy and of "being second rate" were the major problems that motivated them to seek psychotherapy. A clear difference arose between therapists and nontherapists, however, in the area of integrating thoughts and feelings and expressing feelings better: only one therapist stated that this was a necessity as part of her psychotherapy, while a number of nontherapists believed this to be crucial. This may be explained by the amount of professional training in learning to identify feelings and express them skillfully, which many therapists receive as part of their graduate education. Professional training outside the mental health field does not usually include increasing the skillful communication of thoughts and feelings.

Other areas of importance to both groups included being less self-critical and depressed, along the lines Scarf (1980) discusses; increased self-reliance and risk-taking ability; dealing with authority; and leading a "balanced" life. Additionally, a number of therapists were interested in a better understanding of their childhood, themselves, and their relationships in their family of origin, while nontherapists seemed to have less interest in their personal past and more interest in their present and future.

Putting these seemingly disparate elements into a whole, a gestalt begins to emerge: these professional women suffered actively from feelings of personal inadequacy. They sought therapy to learn to be more self-reliant, to deal better with career issues, and to establish meaningful pathways to interpersonal and intergenerational closeness. The therapists believed that they needed to discuss their past to achieve their goals; the nontherapists recognized that they needed to handle feelings more effectively as a means to their goals.

Around issues of role conflicts, all the women expressed

themselves poignantly. Both groups described feeling tempted to nurture business colleagues because they were so used to receiving rewards as nurturers. Both groups described feeling guilty and responsible for business situations that they knew, rationally, to be out of their own control. They felt they were trying to be likeable at the expense of their own career achievement and had great difficulty channeling their aggressiveness and competitiveness constructively. There was overwhelming agreement about the central issues in their psychotherapy: they found it difficult to take themselves and their careers seriously and wanted their psychotherapy to help them become more assertive and more self-reliant. They wanted to be better able to depend on an internal locus of control and to deal with feelings of negativity and hopelessness within a career setting. For example, one woman therapist said, "The closest, most painful issue . . . is learning to realize that a woman has value in her own self, not connected to a husband or a family . . . women must learn to develop a new perspective on their own self-concepts."

Finally, the respondents were asked to address the professional and career-oriented issues that seemed particularly relevant to women. This question enabled them to shift from responding on a feeling level to responding cognitively. As a result, the answers were less poignant, more academic. The major dilemma mentioned was *guilt over role conflict*, which is considered by authors to be a front-runner in personal issues confronting women today (see Friedan, 1981; Kaslow and Schwartz, 1978). Another way of describing this conflict was "leading a balanced life." Using oneself as a basis for identification rather than identifying through relating successfully to others was mentioned next often. A number of women therapists mentioned difficulties in developing as successful career women without personal and professional role models, a problem that follows logically from their statements that their choice of therapist related to finding someone whom they could use as a role model. As one woman said, "Women face choices and decisions . . . that they haven't had to deal with in the past. As a central issue, I see . . . having to figure out a satisfying life course without the solid guidelines available to those raised in traditional roles."

The respondents were asked to reflect on issues in their clients or colleagues that touched them and to consider how they dealt professionally with others who had issues close to their own dilemmas. In general, the same issues were mentioned as in other parts of the questionnaire, notably problems in role confusion and lack of feeling empowered. They found that the identification process with clients or colleagues led to both negative and positive consequences. On the positive side, because the issues in other women's lives seemed so familiar to them, an automatic empathy occurred, which put them into a uniquely positive capacity to help a client or colleague. One businesswoman said, "In my position as a . . . manager . . . I have women and men . . . who report to me. . . . They do remind me of myself . . . I think this similarity helps me to be more sensitive to their needs as their manager."

However, where the issues were too close to ongoing conflicts, the experience was a painful one and became disadvantageous, particularly for the therapists. To be more specific, no nontherapist mentioned identification as a disadvantage; they mentioned identification as an advantage. In the therapist group the identification was seen as both positive and negative. A relevant consideration in understanding the responses is that psychotherapy involves countertransference and transference, making it difficult for therapists to work with clients whose issues are similar to their own unresolved issues. As one therapist said:

> My female clients often remind me of myself. . . . this . . . can be a disadvantage when a client's struggle parallels your own struggle. It's humbling to be reminded of the areas where I still have work to do on myself. I know that I tend to tread more lightly with clients around issues that are not reasonably resolved in myself.

OBSERVATIONS AND FUTURE DIRECTION

Preparing this chapter became analogous to creating a patchwork quilt, an art form entirely created by American women. It started with a collection of "patches" of literature that were not specifically relevant to psychotherapy with women therapists, although pertinent to women, and to psychotherapy. The author's analysis of the responses to the questionnaire became the "thread," based on the thoughts and feelings of a group of professional women with insight into their own processes of development and of change. The "pattern" for the quilt was imposed by the author, but came from the combination of personal responses to the questionnaire and from the literature available. The finished product, the chapter, emerged as a unique statement by a group of capable women, interested in the art of healthy female adult development. An examination of the pattern of these women's statements about themselves, as it related to the literature, led to considerations about the present and the future of psychotherapy with women therapists.

The women therapists clearly and unswervingly stated that they were looking for role models. They indicated that they, like other women professionals, struggled with feeling worthwhile, and that they must fight the seduction of using nurturing as a way of trying to achieve. They need competent women mental health professionals with whom to share their struggles and from whom to learn. In *The Seasons of a Man's Life* (1978, pp. 99–101), Levinson discusses the crucial importance of a mentor relationship. He states that the mentor relationship becomes one of the most complex and developmentally important ones a man can have in early adulthood. He goes on to describe the necessity for the young man to "learn the ropes" from someone whom he can admire and respect and whose career path is similar enough to his own to be that of a role model for him. The young professional man then "apprentices" himself as a fledgling to this person who takes a personal interest in him. Levinson states:

> Women have less mentoring than men. One of the great problems of women is that female mentors are scarce, especially in the world of work. A few women who might serve as mentors are often too beset by the stresses of survival in a work world dominated by men to provide good mentoring for other women.

Levinson continues:

> The mentor represents a mixture of parent and peer; he must be both and not purely either one. His primary function is to be a transitional figure. In early adulthood, a young man must shift from being a child in relation to parental adults to being an adult in a peer relationship with other adults.
>
> Mentoring is best understood as a form of love relationship. In this respect as in others, it is like the intense relationship between parents and grown offspring, or between sexual lovers or spouses. The mentoring relationship lasts perhaps two or three years on the average, eight to ten years at most. Much of its value

may be realized—as in a love relationship generally—after termination. The conclusion of the main phase does not put an end to the meaning of the relationship. Following the separation, the younger man may take the admired qualities of the mentor more fully into himself. He may become better able to learn from himself, to listen to the voices from within. His personality is enriched as he makes his mentor a more intrinsic part of himself. Internalization of significant figures is a major source of development in adulthood.

It is an oversimplification to equate psychotherapy with women therapists to an extension of the mentoring process, even if the therapist chooses a female therapist. There are many other dimensions to the psychotherapy relationship: goals of symptom change, historical understanding of conflict, and a transferential working through of parent-child relationships. What emerges from what the study respondents have stated is that these other facets of psychotherapy are similar for therapists and nontherapists. All the women in this sample chose to work on goals of symptom change; all concentrated on interpersonal conflicts, both in the present and historically; all were concerned with problems of self-image. The major differentiating factor between therapists and nontherapists was that the former, as part of their own therapeutic growth, sought a model very similar to the mentor so well described by Levinson. These women therapists wanted skillful psychotherapy from a person whom they could consider a "transitional figure," someone through whom they could shift from being a professional child in relation to the professional adulthood of the therapist, to being a professional adult, better able to learn from herself through the process of internalization of a significant figure.

Stewart (1977) tested for women the applicability of Levinson's premise that a developmental change occurs about age 30 that culminates in the integration and stabilization of the early adult life structure. Her findings support Levinson's data base with males until age 30, but suggest that women must come to terms with issues of marriage and parenting in a qualitatively and quantitatively different way from men. She states that the ways in which women deal with marriage and parenting affect the mentoring process significantly. Therefore, although this process exists for women, she found that it is more complex, more variable, and more difficult for females, who find that traditionally female goals are not valued in the culture, but that women are sanctioned negatively for not achieving them. Like Erikson (1968, 1974) in his discussion of identity, she speaks of adolescence as a time when young people try on "different hats" in order to find out who they are and who they can become.

It is valuable to consider these developmental concepts in relation to the women therapists involved in the questionnaire. In terms of chronological age, they overlapped with Levinson's period of Early Adulthood, the period during which the male adult shifts from being a "novice" adult to occupying a more established place in adult society. For the nontherapists, psychotherapy provided a relationship-based structure within which previously destructive habits could be changed and personal and professional development could progress with maximal life satisfaction. For the therapists, an added dimension existed. The opportunity to "try on hats" and to view very carefully the "hat" of the therapist heavily influenced their choice of therapist. In asking why a therapist wanted me to be her therapist, I found that a number of reasons were mentioned repeatedly: professional accomplishments (past president, Philadelphia Society of Clinical Psychologists), reputation as a therapist and clinical therapy supervisor, theoretical background in human development from Bryn Mawr College. Of most interest, however, was the repeated statement that my life appeared "full" and "balanced"; that I seemed to combine a varied career with a long-standing marriage and child raising. At times I was told bluntly that the female therapist needed models and wanted me to be one. The sample of women therapists confirm the concepts presented by Levinson (1978) and modified for women by Stewart (1977). And, in their more vulnerable psychological moments, these competent women therapists requested the freedom to be adolescents professionally, in the Eriksonian sense, i.e., to try on personal and professional "hats" within the security of the psychotherapeutic relationship, with a female therapist whose "hat" they were interested in.

In a recent meeting with Carl Whitaker, M.D., and his wife, Muriel Whitaker, Mrs. Whitaker (1983) asked me whether I had ever been in therapy with, or wanted to be in therapy with, a women therapist. I answered that I would be delighted to work with a woman therapist who could model the level of personal power and integrity I was interested in pursuing and that the female mentors I had experience with as a Ph.D. student at Bryn Mawr College were instrumental in the internalization of my sense of integrity and validity as a female and as a professional. The therapists in this sample are asserting a similar drive in choosing their therapists.

If, as was true for me and for the therapists for whom I have been a therapist, younger women look to more senior therapists for modeling, many facets of responsibility rest with the senior female therapist. Competence as a professional, credentials within the professional community, and vibrancy in personal life satisfaction are valuable components of the mentoring process that are likely to be unstated components of the psychotherapy.

In addition, it is crucial that the senior therapist not be seduced by the false heroine worship that goes with the early phases of the mentoring process. If younger female therapists need "heroines," it is crucial that their therapists need not be "heroines." Transferentially, countertransferentially, and in simple human terms, the developmental task of the younger therapist is to introject qualities of the older as a way of coming to terms with who she is and wants to be in her own right.

This seems best achieved by a presentation of self that is both competent and humble. Female psychotherapists need to see their therapist as internally powerful and displaying professional strength and leadership. Seemingly paradoxically, the capacity to experience one's strength also involves the display of one's own fallibility. It is one thing to claim that one is human, and it is another to show it. If therapists are to train other therapists who do not hide behind their books, who are not too afraid to help people tackle the inconsistencies and struggles in their lives, then clinicians must not only be aware of but must also allow their doubts and vulnerabilities to be visible. It is the balance that is of crucial import. Women therapists-in-training reported that it was of great learning value to them to observe that their own therapist did not always behave perfectly and yet continued to confidently and enthusiastically encounter clients and the problems they brought. Perhaps it is this unique combination of strength and fallibility that is a cornerstone in the modeling process. If senior therapists, male or female, can demonstrate this, then clients can learn from it. If the clients are psychotherapists, they can internalize it and later go on to teach it.

Keeping some of these multifaceted issues in focus, psychotherapy with women therapists emerges as a rich and dynamic process operating on a number of levels at any given moment.

From the point of view of being the female therapist, and from the positions described by these women therapists in treatment, the process is a rewarding one, which, however, is desperately lacking research data. For the future, two things seem essential to the responsible continuation of the training of female therapists: first, cross-sectional and longitudinal data about the self-image issues that all these women bring as problems to their own psychotherapy; and second, experienced female clinicians assisting younger female clinicians in becoming models for the "next clinical generation" so that the "modeling gap" continues to narrow.

References

Abroms, G. M. Supervision as metatherapy. In F. W. Kaslow and Associates, *Supervision, consultation, and staff training in the helping professions*. San Francisco: Jossey-Bass, 1977.

American Psychological Association. Counseling women II. *The Counseling Psychologist*, 1976, *6* (2). (Entire issue).

American Psychological Association. Counseling Women III. *The Counseling Psychologist*, 1979, *8* (1). (Entire issue).

Bardwick, J. M. *Psychology of women: A study of the bio-cultural conflicts*. New York: Harper and Row, 1971.

Brodsky, A. M., & Hare-Mustin, R. I. *Women and psychotherapy: An assessment of research and practice*. New York: Guilford Press, 1980.

Cox, R. *Youth into maturity*. New York: Mental Health Materials Center, 1970.

Erikson, E. H. *Identity, youth and crisis*. New York: W. W. Norton, 1968.

Erikson, E. H. Once more the inner space. In Stouse, J. (Ed.), *Women and analysis*. New York: Grossman Publishers, 1974, 820–843.

Franks, V., & Burtle, V. (Eds.). *Women in therapy*. New York: Brunner/Mazel, 1974.

Friedan, B. *The second stage*. New York: Summit Books, 1981.

Garfield, S. L. Research on the training of professional psychotherapists. In A. Gurman and A. Razin (Eds.), *Effective psychotherapy: A handbook of research*. New York: Pergamon Press, 1977.

Garfield, S. L. & Bergin, A. *Handbook of psychotherapy and behavior change*. New York: John Wiley & Sons, 1978.

Gilligan, C. & Norman, M. Woman's place in man's life cycle. Paper presented at the meeting of the Eastern Sociological Association, Philadelphia, March, 1978.

Goldstein, E. Effect of same-sex and cross-sex models on the subsequent academic productivity of scholars. *American Psychologist*, 1979, *34* (5), 407–410.

Gould, R. *Transformations*. New York: Simon and Schuster, 1978.

Gurman, A. & Razin, A. (Eds.). *Effective psychotherapy: A handbook of research*. New York: Pergamon Press, 1977.

Henry, W. E., Sims, J., & Spray, S. L. *Public and private lives of psychotherapists*. San Francisco: Jossey-Bass, 1973.

Issues concerning professional women in health care: Fourth annual conference, Thomas Jefferson University, Philadelphia, March, 1983.

Kaslow, F. W., & Schwartz, L. L. Self-perceptions of the attractive, successful female professional. *Intellect*, February, 1978.

Levinson, D. L. *The seasons of a man's life*. New York: Alfred A. Knopf, 1978.

Maccoby, E., & Jacklin, C. *The psychology of sex differences*. Stanford, California: Stanford University Press, 1974.

Malcolm, J. *Psychoanalysis: The impossible profession.* New York: Vintage Books, 1982.

O'Connell, A. N. Gender-specific barriers to research in psychology: Report of the Task Force on Women Doing Research-APA Division 35. *JSAS Selected Documents in Psychology.* 1978, *1753*, 1–10.

O'Connell, A. N., & Russo, N. F. (Eds.). Eminent women in psychology: Models of achievement. *Psychology of Women Quarterly*, 1980, *5* (1). (Entire issue).

Racusin, G. R., Abramowitz, S. I., & Winter, W. D. Becoming a therapist: Family dynamics and career choice. *Professional Psychology*, 1981, *12* (2), 271–279.

Sank, L. I., & Prout, M. F. Critical issues for the fledgling therapist. *Professional Psychology*, 1978, *9*, 638–645.

Scarf, M. *Unfinished business.* New York: Ballantine Books, 1980.

Stewart, W. A. A psychosocial study of the formation of the early adult life structure in women. (Doctoral dissertation, Columbia University, 1977). *Dissertation Abstracts International*, 1977, *38* (1–B). (University Microfilms, No. 77–14, 849, 163).

Strupp, H. H. The effect of the psychotherapist's personal analysis on his techniques. *Journal of Consulting Psychology*, 1955, *19*, 197–204.

Vaillant, G. *Adaptation to life.* Boston: Little, Brown and Company, 1977.

Welnar, A., Marten, S., Wochnick, E., Davis, M., Fishman, R., & Clayton, P. Psychiatric disorders among professional women. *Archives of General Psychiatry*, 1979, *36*, 169–173.

Whitaker, M. Personal communication, Philadelphia, Jan. 1983.

EDITOR'S COMMENTARY

By and for Female Therapists

Judith Coché's article encompasses a fine review of the literature on therapy for therapists. Her unique perspective as a female therapist sought out by other female therapists—neophyte and experienced—fills a gap in the literature she has reviewed, which is sparse on this subject.

The amount of identification with the therapist as role model of woman and of therapist can be immense and intense. Thus, just as Lazarus and Fay's chapter underscores the powerful impact of the therapist as it is compounded when the person also functions as mentor/teacher and/or supervisor, the same profound nature of the therapist's influence on therapist-patients is described by Coché. How tremendously important then that graduate and professional education programs select carefully and train well those who will play such significant roles in others' lives. And how urgent it is for consumers of therapeutic services to be cognizant of what credentials a therapist should possess, and going beyond that, what to seek in the more amorphous realm of an effective, empathic therapist in terms of ethics, style, and personality.

There is some evidence here that treatment groups for fledgling and experienced therapists are somewhat different from those for other, more usual patients. That therapists utilize it also as a training experience is undeniable. It is also quite likely that they may rationalize their being there as mostly for training and thus try to escape facing intrapsychic and interpersonal problems. One can speculate how safe group members might feel in the context of present and future professional peers. The risk factor might not be as high in such a "stranger" group as it might be in an in-house "colleague" group like that described by E. Coché, but it is a variable that must be dealt with consciously by the therapist. J. Coché alludes to the fact that she is likely to be more active, do more interpretation, and allow a silence to go on longer with a group of therapist-patients than in nontherapist groups. Hopefully some future controlled comparative research will evolve following this descriptive, clinical study.

Her report and discussion seem to affirm the idea that professional women want to "go for it all"; and today are seeking a well-rounded, full life that encompasses a satisfying marriage, family, and career. Some perceive group therapy with a therapist like Dr. Coché, who embodies all of this in her own life, as one pathway to that particular rainbow.

9

Long-Term Telephone Psychotherapy

Kenneth M. Padach, M.D.

The near-maddening pace of technological advances, the development of multitudes of large companies with offices in many major cities, and the weakening of family ties have made the population of the United States one of the most mobile in the world. Lifelong friendships fade with distance, neighborhoods are fragmented, and many children reach college age only after attendance in numerous different school systems.

In the context of this endless circle of motion, the slow but steady development of a therapeutic alliance between therapist and patient is still possible. The relationship, once fragile, untrusting, and superficial can become, over time, strong and productive. Yet, seemingly in an instant, one of the two participants may be whisked off to a distant city. To put this occurrence into proper perspective, it is known that more than 40 million people, constituting over 20 percent of the population of this country, move each year (Zwerling, 1980). That treatment is interrupted by such a circumstance is by no means an isolated event.

The most common reason for transferring patients 20 years ago was the therapeutic impasse resulting from unsurmountable transference-countertransference problems between therapist and patient (Wolberg, 1954). Termination or transfer were the only viable options available. But what does one do when treatment is interrupted prematurely by a move of either therapist or patient? To many, transfer or termination are unacceptable alternatives. However, in the last ten to fifteen years, an alternative has been slowly developing, namely, the use of the telephone for continuing psy-

173

chotherapy when the patient or therapist moves to another locale. This chapter examines the rationale for utilizing the telephone in structured, interpretive, long-term psychotherapy and the unique applicability of this mode of treatment for psychotherapy trainees and practitioners.

LONG-TERM TELEPHONE PSYCHOTHERAPY

When one speaks of continuation of long-term therapy by telephone, one must differentiate between formal and informal procedures in the use of the telephone. Many authors have written on the informal or periodic use of the phone following discontinuation of face-to-face contact (Chiles, 1974; Miller, 1973; Rosenbaum, 1974). The usual procedure is that the patient is allowed to call with no specific time established, and no fee is charged. Presumably, these calls are for "checking in" and follow-up and usually last for less than ten minutes. In a study by Rosenbaum (1977) of 45 analysts who had continued contact with one or more patients, only two had charged fees for the phone sessions. The calls to these two analysts ran more than ten minutes.

There exist two broad classes of telephone usage in psychotherapy:

1. Unstructured, unscheduled, intermittent, fee-free calls that serve the purpose of "touching base" and reassurance that the therapist still exists and cares, and
2. A structured, scheduled, fee-for-service, longer duration call that more closely resembles an actual face-to-face session.

Langs (1974) believes that the first type of call might foster regression, dependence, or acting-out, if abused. I agree and suggest that the structure provided in the second type of call can also avoid the intrusion the therapist might feel from phone calls made on a more impulsive basis. Scheduling the calls and charging a fee is more apt to limit these difficulties and help sustain the objectivity and structure that the therapeutic relationship requires. Whether the therapist should structure continued contact by setting a time and a length for the call with a fee or should permit ad lib contact is a matter for joint decision and responsibility of both the therapist and the patient. Whatever the choice, it must be adhered to lest the abuse of privileges undermine the relationship. Phone sessions henceforth will refer to structured, prearranged appointments for which a fee is charged, similar in mechanics to face-to-face treatment. This is the preferred option when it is important to maintain contact with the same therapist for a continued period of time, especially if uncovering, insight, and interpretive work rather than just supportive care are to be continued.

One may question at the outset whether the telephone can be used at all for long-term psychotherapy. Inherent in this mode of communication are factors that do not normally arise in regular face-to-face sessions. Foremost in this regard is the total lack of available visual cues, leaving communication of feelings and ideas solely in the realm of speech. Since it has been estimated that two-thirds of social meaning is conveyed between two individuals by nonverbal cues (Birdwhistle, 1974), a lack of these cues is likely to intensify the need to listen (Grumet, 1979). Indeed, for adequate communication of emotions to occur, feelings, covert thoughts, and body cues would have to be converted into speech. Wolf (1969) speculated that a large amount of concentration and attention might thus be demanded. It is hypothesized here that if this could be accomplished successfully by patients, a valuable avenue of insight and affectual self-assessment could be developed, giving patients substantially greater access to their feelings. However, if this task is not successfully accomplished, the lack of visual cues could be expected to have a detrimental effect on the interaction.

Without face-to-face contact, there is a tendency toward a decrease in the awareness of reality factors (Wolf, 1969). This may allow visual fantasies by both the patient and therapist to go unchecked and transference to develop more readily (Grumet, 1979; Rosenbaum, 1974). This effect can be likened to the use of the analytic couch to shield the therapist from the patient's view, allowing the latter to fantasize and project without distraction. Thus, the therapist can remain relatively opaque over the phone, and the expression of transference material can be facilitated. However, it has been observed that when telephone participants were deprived of visual cues, anxiety arose that provoked defensive maneuvers in a variety of directions, such as blaming bad telephone reception for not hearing a confrontative comment (Wolf, 1969). Hence, forces facilitating as well as inhibiting expression of sensitive material exist when using the telephone, so that the effect of this stimulus barrier will be different depending on each patient. Those patients made uneasy by the lack of visual cues will be expected to respond with an inhibited expression of sensitive issues, while those more comfortable with the particular arrangement might show an increased willingness to open up.

The spatial arrangements afforded with telephone therapy can offer several distinct advantages over conventional face-to-face therapy. By maintaining a physical distance from the therapist, a sense of safety is created, allowing more vulnerable areas to be revealed (Daniel, 1973). Telephone patients have a unique advantage in being able to control just how much of themselves is revealed. Without the visual cues, the therapist is dependent upon the patient's cooperation to disclose verbally what might otherwise be conveyed through nonverbal behavior. This can present a difficult problem with patients who resist strongly. The opportunity to exclude and elude the therapist successfully is compounded by the use of the phone. A telephone patient has more opportunity to choose just how much to tell the therapist than does someone in a face-to-face session.

The distance offered by the telephone may also help in "shielding" the patient from the therapist during the expression of overwhelming transference affect (Grumet, 1979). Indeed, the telephone might reduce the overwhelming feeling of a powerful transference to an intensity the patient can better tolerate (Saul, 1951). This could allow a more continuous flow of powerful affect, since the patient would not be distracted by the therapist's presence. Particularly in regard to hostile and aggressive emotions, the protection phone therapy offers can facilitate fuller effective expression without the possibility of physical acting on the impulse or fear of immediate physical retaliation by the therapist.

Although the factors just discussed play a significant role when the telephone is the medium for psychotherapy, probably the most substantial and most overlooked reason for continuation of therapy by phone after a premature interruption is the very nature of the therapeutic process; that is, gradually building a therapeutic alliance and slowly uncovering layer upon layer of conflict and defense. It is well established (Keith, 1966; Langs, 1974; Saul, 1951; Wolberg, 1954) that it can take a considerable amount of time before enough trust is established for very sensitive material to emerge. Building a strong therapeutic alliance takes time. Kemble (1941) discusses the development of this alliance; there is minimal intensity of the relationship at the outset, followed by a period of considerable engagement and work, and then a gradual decline in intensity as termination nears. The time that it takes in the therapeutic process to reach the middle work phase and the depths of exploration to which it can transcend is contingent on many factors, including resistances of the patient, his or her rate of change, the magnitude of the problems, and the degree and manner with which the therapist participates and his or her therapeutic skill. Rather than prematurely terminating treatment while the patient is in this work phase, especially if it has taken a long time to arrive at this stage, the patient should have the opportunity to continue by telephone to maximize the benefits of that laboriously developed alliance. When a patient has exceptional rapport with the therapist, the time required to begin again and to develop such a relationship, if at all, with a different therapist must be weighed with the few disadvantages of continuation by telephone. If the limitations of phone therapy are kept in mind, the continuing relationship can provide the additional necessary time to maximize the work that can be done. For those patients who have been in productive therapy for years, the option of continuing that fruitful relationship is not only warranted, but advantageous. The consistency achieved by keeping that same relationship throughout treatment is well worth the price paid for not being able to continue in person.

LONG-TERM TELEPHONE THERAPY FOR THERAPISTS

This brings me to the area of discussion around which this text is focused, namely, *psychotherapy with psychotherapists*. In by far the majority of cases, students pursuing careers in the mental health field, regardless of what discipline of training they enter, must move several times during their training. High school may be in one town, college in another. Then graduate school, practice and/or internship come, followed by residency and possibly a fellowship, all usually in different locations. Psychotherapy trainees are vulnerable to premature rupture of their therapy because they are often assigned to more advanced students in clinics; this can mean turnover from either side of the therapy-therapist pairing. For a psychiatry resident, telephone therapy might be a viable consideration to preclude the necessity of changing therapists every year when the senior resident moves on. The possibility of being able to maintain face-to-face contact with the same therapist throughout an extended period of training is at best exiguous. Of course, transfer should be effected when a change of therapist is warranted and when there are no compelling reasons for continuing the existing alliance. (This is discussed later in detail.)

It is expected that graduate therapists will have worked out their own conflicts to a point where these will not surface to interfere with their work. This can take time, time that can be realized using telephone therapy. Likewise, it can be tremendously beneficial to be exposed to a long-term treatment relationship in one's own therapy to see how such a relationship develops and changes and why it can take a long time to do so while still being valuable throughout; it provides an excellent en vivo model of the therapeutic relationship and process.

Another option phone therapy can provide for trainees especially, but also for other patients, is the opportunity for periodic, "crisis oriented" treatment *with the original therapist*. In these situations, the therapeutic alliance has long been established. Similarly, senior graduate clinicians may choose to go into therapy for a second, third, or even fourth time, to work on issues not dealt with in the past or on new ones that have arisen. The benefit of picking up with the original therapist and having the treatment relationship already firmly established can save considerable time and money, in addition to providing valuable continuity in treatment. The thought of the time and effort required to establish a new relationship could serve as a deterrent, while this process might encourage therapists to seek brief treatment for minor issues.

Case Presentation

Let me now present a case that illustrates many issues discussed in this chapter.

F. is a 34-year-old social worker who is an only child. F.'s mother is a distant, compulsive woman who never showed much affection. Her father is an insurance executive who is intelligent, hard working, but also unavailable.

After a relatively atraumatic childhood, F. entered school, where she excelled. She was fiercely independent and chose not to confide in anyone, never having a best friend. Her first serious sex-

ual relationship was at age 17 and lasted two years. It, like her subsequent relationships, was characterized by rapid attachment,
clinging and mutual dependency, perfectionism, and immediate
withdrawal at the first sign of threatened loss. The breakup of this
relationship precipitated a serious depression, and she saw a college counselor for one year, twice monthly, and terminated treatment on the grounds that "everything was worked out." Following
the disruption of a subsequent relationship, F. again became depressed and began using drugs. She then entered weekly therapy
with a psychiatrist for fourteen months. This ended when F. grad-
uated from college and relocated in another city, again feeling that
everything had been resolved.

After several years of working, F. realized that she was still experiencing considerable difficulties in her life and entered treatment with Dr. H., a female psychologist. During the next sixteen
months, it became apparent that F. had the following conflicts: extreme perfectionistic attitude, depression with tremendous difficulty expressing anger, and a relationship history characterized by
dependency and enormous separation anxiety.

During the months of face-to-face therapy, excellent rapport
was established and some good exploration of some superficial issues ensued. However, F. was unable to explore fully any dependency or aggressiveness issues. Sexual themes were touched upon
but again not explored fully because of F.'s sexual ambivalence and
inhibition about discussing this very personal issue. When it became known that Dr. H. was to leave town to take an appointment
in another city, the therapy sessions were flooded with new material in an attempt to stop the termination. For once, it was not F.
who was ending the relationship. It was now out of her control. In
lieu of the past history of difficulties in ending relationships and
flights from therapy, and also in consideration of the excellent rapport that had developed, Dr. H. suggested the possibility of continuing therapy by telephone. F. did not want to transfer to another therapist, for she did not feel that she could again readily
establish such a strong and meaningful alliance as she had with Dr.
H. She also, for the first time, was able to admit that her treatment
was not finished and that she desired to continue. It was agreed to
continue weekly 50-minute sessions over the phone with the same
fee.

Therapy continued for two more years, weekly for the first
year, then irregularly (once or twice a month) in the second year as

issues would come up. F. reached the point where she worked intensely on her own between sessions and would arrange a call with Dr. H. when she needed clarification.

What happened to the therapy after switching to the phone deserves special attention. It was anticipated that the disruption of the relationship, at the time of the move, might set off severe depression. What followed in the months of telephone therapy was F.'s ability to express directly to Dr. H. her intense rage at Dr. H.'s leaving her and F.'s overwhelming fear of being abandoned. For the first time, F. was able to see that her rage would not destroy the other person or the relationship and that warm, close feelings still existed underneath.

With the safety provided by the distance of the telephone, F. was able to discuss her wish to be cared for by Dr. H., which enabled an avalanche of preoedipal material to emerge. F. said herself that she felt much safer expressing these feelings over the phone and would not likely have done so in person. With the relationship able to last the length of time that it did, F. eventually began to see her dependence on Dr. H., which had been denied to this point. In time, she was able to accept it and eventually work it through, being aware of the acceptance, support, and continued interest of her therapist in her fine progress.

INDICATIONS FOR LONG-TERM
TELEPHONE PSYCHOTHERAPY

This case illustrates several general situations where continuation of treatment by telephone might be useful. A first area of consideration pro phone therapy is that of separation anxiety and object loss. Pumpian-Mindlin (1958) describes three types of patients with respect to various amounts of separation anxiety and how a transfer might affect them. Type 1 patients are those with little separation anxiety to whom a transfer would be rather benign. With these patients, there seems to be little attachment to the particular therapist. They may be more attached to the clinic (Reider, 1953). Type 2 patients are those with moderate separation anxiety in whom a transfer will create definite difficulties. He suggests that preliminary arrangements, including an appointment, should be made with a specific therapist. The majority of patients fit into this category. Type 3 patients are those with marked separation anxiety in whom transfer will create serious problems. He suggests arranging a joint meeting with the new therapist to introduce the patient and try to prevent premature rupture of treatment at a time when termination is contraindicated, thus aborting a flight into a hospital or severe regression.

I agree with Pumpian-Mindlin on the first group of patients, but disagree with him as to the treatment of the latter two groups. Most strikingly, in the third group is the possibility that the transfer will have a negative therapeutic effect in that the patient may resort to utilizing earlier ineffective defensive patterns to deal with the separation. This may include a suicidal gesture or attempt, marked regression, need for hospitalization and/or any number of pathological defense mechanisms to deal with the stress to which the patient is incapable of adapting. The opportunity to face and cope with this separation by continuing therapy through the phone lets the patient deal with his or her feelings *directly* with that very person whom he or she is losing and, more importantly, with that person with whom he or she has a solidly established therapeutic alliance. The opportunity to challenge the feelings of rejection and abandonment can only be enhanced when confrontation is with that very object one has lost. I would put the social worker in the case cited earlier into this third group, since her object loss history is quite traumatic. For that large second group, I would recommend examining the probability of how each patient will handle the transfer, given his or her object loss history. If that history is traumatic, I would recommend continuation by telephone, if only to work through adequately the impending object loss. If that is successful, transfer might be implemented later.

A comparable argument can be brought to bear when the patient has problems of object constancy and tenuous object relations. The patient without an integrated sense of object constancy needs a therapeutic relationship that will endure over an extended period of time. For our social worker, who was already on her third therapist, there was minimal possibility of maintaining a therapeutic relationship over sufficient time to allow a high enough level of trust to develop so that deeply repressed material could emerge. One cannot add up individual time spent with consecutive therapists. Likewise, those patients with tenuous object relationships, who have difficulty establishing and maintaining relationships, may have built a truly special relationship with their therapist. The opportunity of maintaining this relationship, even if only by telephone, can have lasting therapeutic gains for that patient and his or her future relationships. Certain borderline and narcissistic patients could be considered here, as well as chronic schizophrenics.

There exist specific situations when telephone therapy might not only be considered, but may actually be the treatment of choice. Ambivalent patients, such as some schizophrenics, dealing with the issue of closeness versus distance, or hostile and controlling patients, who need a safe distance in order to express hostility, may find phone therapy a superior medium in which to work (Miller, 1973; Grumet, 1979). The obsessional or schizoid patient may find appealing the impersonal property of the telephone together with the dependence on verbal communication (Miller, 1973). Those individuals fearing face-to-face experiences might more productively use the telephone, which enhances their control over the situation (Daniel, 1973). Chronically depressed individuals might be better able to break out of isolation using the "action-at-a-distance" quality of the telephone versus more strenuous face-to-face contact. In those patients for whom the transference issues are too intense to be dealt with in person, using the telephone may help to dilute the intensity and expedite expression (Saul, 1951). Finally, although this chapter deals with psychotherapy of the uncovering and insight genre, I will just mention continued, long-term, supportive therapy by telephone for following discharged alcoholics (Catanzaro & Green, 1970) and discharged psychiatric patients (Cantanzaro, 1971), and counseling homosexuals (Lester & Brockopp, 1973), to name a few possibilities.

CONTRAINDICATIONS TO LONG-TERM TELEPHONE THERAPY

The discussion of contraindications to long-term telephone therapy necessarily centers around the issues of transference and countertransference. Since the potential for misuse of this mode of therapy owing to countertransference is considerable, it is taken up separately subsequent to this discussion.

Foremost in regard to transference issues is the threat of fostering excessive dependence on the therapist (Kemble, 1941; MacKinnon and Michels, 1970; Miller, 1973). Whether this is desirable and appropriate to the therapist's and patient's treatment goals needs to be evaluated. In the case presented, the dependency needs were not only gratified, they were encouraged. What was crucial for this strategy to be effective was to have a relationship that could endure until such time as F. was able to face and work through these needs. But, if this is not done properly, inappropriate narcissistic demands of the patient may be gratified and grandiose or infantile fantasies may be promoted (Langs, 1974). Tendencies of the patient to regress as treatment time runs out in order to undo the planned ending should be taken as just that and not misinterpreted as a decline in the patient's functioning. Granted, the thrust of this chapter is that therapists should judiciously "keep their doors open" to patients, but a blanket open-door policy can only invite clinging and dependent behavior.

Langs (1974) suggests several other issues that apply to transference reactions specific to the patient's wish to continue treatment with the departing therapist. These include the patient's pathological wish for control over the therapist, especially if it occurs when it is the therapist's departure that forces the break in the treatment relationship. Also, the patient may resort to omnipotent denial of the impending loss. Gratifying requests to continue treatment based on these issues without prior close scrutiny can make it extremely difficult to work these issues through in subsequent treatment.

A few final points on the contraindications to phone therapy illustrate some of the more practical limitations of its use. Patients who have difficulty articulating their feelings and thoughts are poor candidates for treatment over the phone. Likewise, those patients with fragile reality testing who need the visual input face-to-face therapy provides will not be likely to profit from phone therapy. Last but not least, there must exist a willingness on the part of the patient (and the therapist) to translate their nonverbal behavior and covert thoughts into speech. Without this ability, too much valuable material will be lost.

Another important contraindication for phone therapy can emanate from countertransference issues. There are those therapists, especially among those medically trained, who need the "laying on of the hands" aspect of face-to-face therapy in order to feel effective (Pisani, 1968). In a study comparing initial interviews done by telephone with those conducted face-to-face (Antonioni, 1973), it was found that therapists preferred face-to-face contact while patients found it easier to talk about their conflicts over the phone. Miller and Beebe (Miller, 1973), studying 58 psychiatrists, found that 38 percent of them found the telephone easy to use as a mode of communication, 45 percent were equivocal in their responses, and 16 percent found it difficult to use. That so many therapists found the modality unsatisfactory may reflect a feeling of loss of control by the therapist, who is unable to see the patient, and a frustration at the distance of the patient. It is a bias of many therapists that contact by the telephone, initiated by the patient, is a manifestation of resistance (MacKinnon & Michels, 1970). Although sometimes this may be true, it might help at times to permit this resistance in the hope of allowing more sensitive material to emerge.

A second controversial countertransference issue centers around the therapist's feelings about the premature interruption of therapy and how he or she might inappropriately choose to atone by continuing treatment by telephone. If it is the therapist who must leave the relationship, a sense of guilt may arise over "deserting his patients" (Dewald, 1965). On the other hand, if it is the patient who must leave the relationship, the therapist may feel betrayed insofar as he or she had invested so much in the relationship and will not be able to see it through. Therapists must deal with their own separation anxieties. Indeed, it is possible to see the therapist experience symptomatic manifestations of object loss concomitantly with the patient (Keith, 1966). The therapist may be overly possessive of the patient and be unable to let go (Kemble, 1941). Inability of the therapist to deal with the patient's anger, overidentification with the patient, or the need to feel that his or her work is so important that treatment could not possibly end at the time of interruption can all affect the therapist's judgment (Dewald, 1965). If any or all of the above predicaments exist, the therapist must endeavor to deal with these feelings adequately and objectively in order to be in a position to decide if telephone therapy is a better course to pursue than transfer or termination.

In a study of forced interruptions of therapy with psychiatric residents, Pumpian-Mindlin (1958) found a direct correlation between the negative attitude of therapists towards their next assignment and their ability to deal with terminations or transfers adequately, in that the more reluctant the therapist was to take the next assignment, the more difficulty there was in separating from the patients. Keith (1966) delineates a "Transfer Syndrome" among residents facing interruption of treatment that includes:

1. denial—through delay in telling the patient about the impending separation, leaving too little time to resolve conflicts,
2. self-denigration—devaluing the therapist's own effectiveness with the patient, and
3. losing sight of the therapeutic process—the therapist feels guilty that the treatment goals have not been reached.

This last point may be exaggerated by the therapist who assumes automatically that the patient needs continuing treatment (Dewald, 1965), distorting the picture of the patient's total functioning through underestimating the patient's ego strengths and overestimating the degree of malfunctioning (Pumpian-Mindlin, 1958).

Another point about countertransference is raised by Scher (1970) regarding the relationship of the patient with the new therapist. When the patient is transferred, he or she is likely to talk a great deal about the old therapist to the new therapist, perhaps distortedly, with little chance of defense for the former therapist. Knowing this will occur may influence the old therapist when recommending a replacement. The potential therapist, on the other hand, may find that he or she does not want to see this patient and hear about a friend or colleague through the patient's comments, thus, perhaps, being forced to reject the patient at a time when the patient is still recovering from separation from the old therapist.

THE TRANSFER PROCESS

It would be beneficial at this time to examine the transfer process itself. Specifically, what are some potential negative and positive consequences of a transfer following a premature rupture of therapy? First and foremost is whether the transfer will, in fact, take root. Keith (1966) raises two questions on this issue: will the patient be able to grieve over the departing therapist? and will the patient try to persuade the departing and replacement therapists that the problems that brought the patient to treatment no longer exist and that termination is in order instead? A second problem is presented by Feldman (1968), who reports of circumstances, although rare, of strong positive transference to the original therapist making transfer difficult, if not impossible. In this event, if the patient accepts the idea of transfer, he or she may not follow through, and some patients may even decompensate over the loss and need to be hospitalized (Rosenbaum, 1974).

Scher (1970) describes a therapeutic triangle that can develop between the departing therapist, the patient, and the new therapist. The patient may feel uncontrollably exposed to the new therapist, especially if the previous therapist tries to aid the transfer by sharing information about the patient with the new therapist. The patient may have no control over how much is revealed to the stranger therapist. To complicate matters even further, the patient may succumb to a dilemma: if he or she gets better, there may be feelings of disloyalty to the former therapist; if he or she gets worse, there may be the feeling of having failed the very person who rescued him or her from desertion; and if he or she stays the same, all three are defeated. "For better or for worse, the interaction between the patient and his new therapist will forever be influenced by the relationship which each of them had with the departing therapist" (Scher, 1970, p. 282).

A final perplexing issue is that of the disconnected nature of therapy some patients receive, especially those who are being treated at teaching institutions or training facilities where patient transfers are a common occurrence (Keith, 1966) at the end of each academic year or trainee rotation. Although it has been suggested (Reider, 1953) that some patients might be better able to tolerate this stress by forming their attachment with the institution or agency rather than with the specific therapist, those patients being seen privately cannot use this option. It must be remembered that transfer to another therapist involves ending with the original therapist (Pumpian-Mindlin, 1958) and that clumsy, unwanted terminations that predate completion of therapy may often nullify therapeutic gains (Kemble, 1941).

Now that potential risks of patient transfers have been discussed, it is also essential to recognize that transfer need not be looked upon only as an unfortunate but inescapable happenstance. Indeed, it has the potential of becoming a critical therapeutic event, allowing an opportunity for the patient to reexperience, rework, and resolve earlier object losses (Scher, 1970). The new therapist should use the opportunity created by the transfer to explore feelings about separation from previous significant others in addition to the therapist, including anger, rejection and abandonment, and loss. By no means is the opportunity to do this limited

to change of therapists occasioned by transfers because of relocation. Feldman (1968) reports that some patients find it advantageous to change therapists and then compare them. A stagnant or
sluggish therapeutic process might be rejuvenated with a new relationship.

A distinct but related issue is the rotation of student therapists
while in training. It was stated earlier how such an experience can
be detrimental to the clinic patient. Here the priorities between
training benefits and therapeutic gains must be carefully considered and weighed. For example, how is a trainee to learn to treat a
diverse population of patients with a myriad array of therapeutic
experience and exposure to different modalities and, at the same
time, give the patient the opportunity to work over the extended
period of time necessary to resolve sensitive and complex issues?
With the rotation system now in practice, the former is accomplished, but at the price of discontinuity of therapy for both the patient and therapist. This disconnectedness the patient and therapist experience can only increase with the diversification and
subspecialization that psychotherapeutic practice is currently experiencing. Transfering patients, then, is not a benign procedure;
if not handled properly, potentially serious consequences may en-
sue and do, sometimes, even if handled properly. Indeed, a termination or transfer might be the most antitherapeutic event a patient
can experience if unable to work through his or her rage and feeling of rejection (Langs, 1974).

PRACTICAL ISSUES

I would like to close with a discussion of some practical issues inherent in the use of the telephone in psychotherapy. The first issue
is that of third-party payment for telephone treatment. In one case
I know, a private insurance company refused to pay for telephone
sessions between a graduate student, who moved to pursue her
educational goals, and her analytically oriented psychiatrist in her
former home town. It was stated that, "Psychotherapy by telephone is not necessary to medical care of illness. By not necessary
we mean any service or supply that is not commonly and customarily recognized throughout the doctor's profession as appropriate
in the treatment of the patient's sickness. . . . psychotherapy

should be face-to-face, direct, personal contact between the patient and the physician at the same physical location, . . ." (anonymous, 1982).

Mental health professionals must address this issue formally so that a policy can be established asserting that telephone therapy can be effective, warranted, and accepted practice under certain circumstances when transfer or termination are contraindicated. Until such a stance is taken, the effect of nonreimbursement for this kind of treatment will be to hinder its development and use.

The second issue of feasibility centers around the needs of the mental health or psychiatric clinic. If therapists, whether trainees or not, were to "take" patients with them through continuation by telephone when they left the clinic, the clinic might suffer financially. This, too, may discourage use of this mode of treatment. In a similar regard, however, a community suffering from a lack of available treatment-time could benefit from such a shift of patients. Patients could well be presented with the options of transfer, termination, or continuation with their therapist and be permitted to participate in the decision making—for one of the ultimate goals of therapy is enabling patients to be more self-directing.

Last is the issue of professional ethics. Is telephone therapy ethical? There is no mention of telephone therapy in the ethical principles for psychiatrists (APA, 1973) nor, to my knowledge, for the other mental health disciplines. Perhaps this idea is still too novel. The only question I can see being raised is whether psychotherapy, which is a one-to-one human relationship, is violated by the telephone being between the participants. I feel that it is not. Granted, telephone therapy is not for everyone. Nevertheless, for those who can benefit from its use, it provides another alternative route to that final common goal of all therapies, improved mental health.

References

American Psychiatric Association. The principals of medical ethics with annotations especially applicable to psychiatry. *American Journal of Psychiatry*, 1973, *130*, 1057–1064.

Anonymous female graduate student, personal conversation, 1982.

Antonioni, D. T. A field study comparison of counselor empathy, concreteness and client self-exploration in face-to-face and telephone counseling during first and second interviews (Doctoral dissertation, University of Wisconsin, 1973). *Dissertation Abstracts International*, 1973, *34*, 866B.

Birdwhistle, R. The language of the body: The natural environment of words. In J. Wiley (Ed.), *Human Communications*. New York: 1974.

Catanzaro, R. J. Telephone therapy. In J. Masserman (Ed.), *Current Psychiatric Therapies* (Vol. 2). New York: Grune & Stratton, 1971.

Catanzaro, R. J., & Green, W. G. WATS telephone therapy: New follow-up techniques for alcoholics. *American Journal of Psychiatry*, 1970, *126*(7), 1024–1027.

Chiles, J. A. A practical therapeutic use of the telephone. *American Journal of Psychiatry*, 1974, *131*(9), 1030–1031.

Daniel, L. B. A study of the influence of introversion-extroversion and neuroticism in telephone counseling versus face-to-face counseling (Doctoral dissertation, University of Texas at Austin, 1973). *Dissertation Abstracts International*, 1973, *34*, 2300B.

Dewald, P. A. Reactions to the forced termination of therapy. *Psychiatric Quarterly*, 1965, *39*, 103–126.

Feldman, F. Results of psychoanalysis in clinic case assignments. *Journal of the American Psychoanalytic Association*, 1968, *16*, 274–279.

Grumet, G. W. Telephone therapy: A review and case study. *American Journal of Orthopsychiatry*, 1970, *49*(4), 574–584.

Keith, C. Multiple transfers of psychotherapy patients. *Archives of General Psychiatry*, 1966, *14*, 185–189.

Kemble, R. P. Constructive use of the ending of treatment. *American Journal of Orthopsychiatry*, 1941, *11*, 684–690.

Langs, R. *The Technique of Psychoanalytic Psychotherapy*, Vol. 2. New York: J. Aranson, 1974.

Lester, D., & Brockopp, G. (Eds.). *Crisis Intervention and Counseling by Telephone*. Springfield, Ill.: Charles C. Thomas, 1973.

MacKinnon, R. A., & Michels, R. The role of the telephone in the psychiatric interview. *Psychiatry*, 1970, *33*, 82–93.

Miller, W. B. The telephone in outpatient psychotherapy. *American Journal of Psychotherapy*, 1973, *27*, 15–26.

Pumpian-Mindlin, E. Comments on techniques of termination and transfer in a clinic setting. *American Journal of Psychotherapy*, 1958, *12*, 455–464.

Pisani, V. Telephone therapy with alcoholics. In G. Mastrangelo (Ed.),

Collected Papers. Milan, Italy: International Institute on Alcoholism, 1968.

Reider, N. A type of transfer to institutions. *Bulletin of the Menninger Clinic*, 1953, *17*, 58–63.

Rosenbaum, M. Continuation of psychotherapy by 'long distance' telephone. *International Journal of Psychoanalytic Psychotherapy*, 1974, *3*, 483–495.

Rosenbaum, M. Premature interruption of psychotherapy: Continuation of contact by telephone and correspondence. *American Journal of Psychiatry, 1977, 134*(2), 200–202.

Saul, L. J. A note on the telephone as a technical aid. *Psychoanalytic Quarterly*, 1951, *20*, 287–291.

Scher, M. The process of changing therapists. *American Journal of Psychotherapy*, 1970, *24*, 278–286.

Wolberg, L. *The Technique of Psychotherapy*. New York: Grune & Stratton, 1954.

Wolf, A. Training in psychoanalysis in groups without face-to-face contact. *American Journal of Psychotherapy*, 1969, *23*, 488–495.

Zwerling, I. Struggle for survival. In *The American Family*. Philadelphia: Smith, Kline and French Laboratories, 1980.

EDITOR'S COMMENTARY

The Efficacy of
a Very Special Phone Connection

Padach presents a persuasive case for the judicious use of telephone therapy as an alternative to termination or transfer when patient or therapist relocate. Padach's discussion challenges the reader to rethink the kind of rigid dictum against this practice that is prevalent in many professional training programs and institutes and which is certainly valid for some patients at some times; but not for all patients at all times. There may be compelling reasons to continue the particular therapeutic alliance, such as when a patient has already had several therapists and would respond poorly to one more abandonment or when disruption of the process at a crucial phase would be detrimental and precipitate a set-back of many months. The therapist's decision that neither termination nor transfer is advisable is not always an inability to let go, or a refusal to recognize that another therapist may also offer the patient excellent treatment.

In my own experience, when I relocated from Pennsylvania to Florida several years ago, I terminated or transferred 95 percent of my patients. But two were deeply involved in profound transference relationships and dealing with extremely charged content that we had been working to release for a long time. The clinical data militated against transfer. Subsequently, one of the patients, a bright and handsome male in his late twenties, was able to deal with heavily laden sexual issues surrounding masturbation, the desire for and fear of homosexuality, and the sometimes intense and extreme behavior he exhibited in sexualized heterosexual relationships. He spontaneously indicated how much more comfortable he was dealing with this material behind the protective screen afforded by the phone than he would have been in person. After numerous sessions devoted to sexual themes, during which he reached some insight and resolution as to how he now wished to comport himself, he stated that he thought he might have been too embarrassed and overwhelmed to ever have gotten to this material in face-to-face treatment.

About a year later, a male psychologist I had been treating for several months on a biweekly basis for double sessions—because of the long distance between my office and his home town—called to say that he was extremely busy and could not spare the extra hours for commuting that week. He wondered if I would be willing to allocate his regularly appointed time for a telephone session instead, since he did not wish to cancel. His request seemed legitimate and not like an attempt to manipulate, and I concurred. Although he had abreacted the traumatic death of his younger sister and completed his delayed bereavement work, and worked intensively on attachment and individuation from his family of origin, he had not considered his dating and other peer-level interpersonal relationships a problem. Here, too, as in the case cited above, a tremendous amount of overt sexual material poured forth during the phone session—ambivalence about the orgies he frequented and his bisexuality. At the close of the phone hour, he volunteered that he had not planned to discuss this today, but somehow the safety provided by not being visible was the trigger which unleashed this content that he had felt too ashamed and frightened to share earlier—especially since, despite the different locales in which we live, we are still part of the same professional network.

I was intrigued by the similarity in the utilization of the phone sessions and by the patients' interpretation of why it became possible for the sexual material to surface in this form. In both instances, considerable relief from their gender identity confusion was experienced and greater clarity and comfort achieved. Also, it caused me to wonder whether I had inhibited their expression of this material in vivo and I shared this question with them. Neither of them thought so and since numerous other male patients have been able to bring up sexual concerns, I discarded this hypothesis. Although an n of 2 is too small for any generalized statement, these clinical deductions regarding the efficacy of telephone therapy raise further the possibilities for the utilization of telephone therapy. Not only can this be an alternative to termination or transfer, but it can be a way to afford safe distance when particularly difficult issues need attention. And, perhaps, it can be used by geographically isolated or nonambulatory individuals who find accessibility to therapists quite limited.

The economic issues Padach alludes to will need to be debated and resolved if this form of therapy is to become accepted as feasible. Is it ethical and just for an agency or institution to cling to patients whose therapeutic progress might be better if they continued by phone with their departing therapist? Who is to make this de-termination a priori? The potential loss in agency income may be the "bottom line" concern rationalized by arguments against the efficacy of phone therapy. Another dilemma is the lack of insurance reimbursement for phone therapy. But perhaps this, too, could be overcome if the major professional associations were to agree that phone therapy is another viable modality in our treatment armamentarium.

Index